W9-AXZ-570

SLEEP

GENERAL EDITORS

Dale C. Garell, M.D.
Medical Director, California Children Services, Department of Health
    Services, County of Los Angeles
Associate Dean for Curriculum; Clinical Professor, Department of Pediatrics &
    Family Medicine, University of Southern California School of Medicine
Former President, Society for Adolescent Medicine

Solomon H. Snyder, M.D.
Distinguished Service Professor of Neuroscience, Pharmacology, and
    Psychiatry, Johns Hopkins University School of Medicine
Former President, Society for Neuroscience
Albert Lasker Award in Medical Research, 1978

CONSULTING EDITORS

Robert W. Blum, M.D., Ph.D.
Associate Professor, School of Public Health and Department of
    Pediatrics
Director, Adolescent Health Program, University of Minnesota
    Consultant, World Health Organization

Charles E. Irwin, Jr., M.D.
Associate Professor of Pediatrics; Director, Division of Adolescent
    Medicine, University of California, San Francisco

Lloyd J. Kolbe, Ph.D.
Chief, Office of School Health & Special Projects, Center for Health
    Promotion & Education, Centers for Disease Control
President, American School Health Association

Jordan J. Popkin
Director, Division of Federal Employee Occupational Health, U.S. Public
    Health Service Region I

Joseph L. Rauh, M.D.
Professor of Pediatrics and Medicine, Adolescent Medicine, Children's
    Hospital Medical Center, Cincinnati
Former President, Society for Adolescent Medicine

THE ENCYCLOPEDIA OF
H E A L T H

THE HEALTHY BODY

Dale C. Garell, M.D. · General Editor

SLEEP

Edward Edelson

Introduction by C. Everett Koop, M.D., Sc.D.

former Surgeon General, U. S. Public Health Service

CHELSEA HOUSE PUBLISHERS

New York · Philadelphia

The goal of the ENCYCLOPEDIA OF HEALTH *is to provide general information in the ever-changing areas of physiology, psychology, and related medical issues. The titles in this series are not intended to take the place of the professional advice of a physician or other health care professional.*

ON THE COVER Sequence of thermographs showing change in skin temperature of a sleeping man. White represents the highest degree of heat; temperatures decrease through red, yellow, and blue, to black, the coolest.

CHELSEA HOUSE PUBLISHERS
EDITOR-IN-CHIEF   Remmel Nunn
MANAGING EDITOR   Karyn Gullen Browne
COPY CHIEF   Mark Rifkin
PICTURE EDITOR   Adrian G. Allen
ART DIRECTOR   Maria Epes
ASSISTANT ART DIRECTOR   Noreen Romano
MANUFACTURING MANAGER   Gerald Levine
SYSTEMS MANAGER   Lindsey Ottman
PRODUCTION MANAGER   Joseph Romano
PRODUCTION COORDINATOR   Marie Claire Cebrián

The Encyclopedia of Health
SENIOR EDITOR   Brian Feinberg

Staff for SLEEP
ASSOCIATE EDITOR   LaVonne Carlson-Finnerty
COPY EDITOR   Christopher Duffy
EDITORIAL ASSISTANT   Tamar Levovitz
PICTURE RESEARCHERS   Sandy Jones and Bill Rice
DESIGNER   Robert Yaffe

3   5   7   9   8   6   4   2

Library of Congress Cataloging-in-Publication Data

Edelson, Edward,
   Sleep/by Edward Edelson; introduction by C. Everett Koop.
   p. cm.—(The Encyclopedia of health. Psychological disorders and their treatment)
   Includes bibliographical references and index.
   Summary: Examines the function of sleep in both humans and animals. Discusses REM sleep, dreams, insomnia, narcolepsy, and other sleep disorders.
   ISBN 0-7910-0092-3
         0-7910-0825-8 (pbk.)
   1. Sleep—Juvenile literature. [1. Sleep.] I. Title II. Series.   91-9279
QP425.E29 1991   CIP
612.8'21—dc20   AC

CONTENTS

THE ENCYCLOPEDIA OF
H E A L T H

THE HEALTHY BODY

The Circulatory System
Dental Health
The Digestive System
The Endocrine System
Exercise
Genetics & Heredity
The Human Body: An Overview
Hygiene
The Immune System
Memory & Learning
The Musculoskeletal System
The Nervous System
Nutrition
The Reproductive System
The Respiratory System
The Senses
Sleep
Speech & Hearing
Sports Medicine
Vision
Vitamins & Minerals

THE LIFE CYCLE

Adolescence
Adulthood
Aging
Childhood
Death & Dying
The Family
Friendship & Love
Pregnancy & Birth

MEDICAL ISSUES

Careers in Health Care
Environmental Health
Folk Medicine
Health Care Delivery
Holistic Medicine
Medical Ethics
Medical Fakes & Frauds
Medical Technology
Medicine & the Law
Occupational Health
Public Health

PSYCHOLOGICAL DISORDERS AND THEIR TREATMENT

Anxiety & Phobias
Child Abuse
Compulsive Behavior
Delinquency & Criminal Behavior
Depression
Diagnosing & Treating Mental Illness
Eating Habits & Disorders
Learning Disabilities
Mental Retardation
Personality Disorders
Schizophrenia
Stress Management
Suicide

MEDICAL DISORDERS AND THEIR TREATMENT

AIDS
Allergies
Alzheimer's Disease
Arthritis
Birth Defects
Cancer
The Common Cold
Diabetes
Emergency Medicine
Gynecological Disorders
Headaches
The Hospital
Kidney Disorders
Medical Diagnosis
The Mind-Body Connection
Mononucleosis and Other Infectious Diseases
Nuclear Medicine
Organ Transplants
Pain
Physical Handicaps
Poisons & Toxins
Prescription & OTC Drugs
Sexually Transmitted Diseases
Skin Disorders
Stroke & Heart Disease
Substance Abuse
Tropical Medicine

PREVENTION AND EDUCATION: THE KEYS TO GOOD HEALTH

C. Everett Koop, M.D., Sc.D.
former Surgeon General,
U.S. Public Health Service

The issue of health education has received particular attention in recent years because of the presence of AIDS in the news. But our response to this particular tragedy points up a number of broader issues that doctors, public health officials, educators, and the public face. In particular, it points up the necessity for sound health education for citizens of all ages.

Over the past 25 years this country has been able to bring about dramatic declines in the death rates for heart disease, stroke, accidents, and for people under the age of 45, cancer. Today, Americans generally eat better and take better care of themselves than ever before. Thus, with the help of modern science and technology, they have a better chance of surviving serious—even catastrophic—illnesses. That's the good news.

But, like every phonograph record, there's a flip side, and one with special significance for young adults. According to a report issued in 1979 by Dr. Julius Richmond, my predecessor as Surgeon General, Americans aged 15 to 24 had a higher death rate in 1979 than they did 20 years earlier. The causes: violent death and injury, alcohol and drug abuse, unwanted pregnancies, and sexually transmitted diseases. Adolescents are particularly vulnerable because they are beginning to explore their own sexuality and perhaps to experiment with drugs. The need for educating young people is critical, and the price of neglect is high.

Yet even for the population as a whole, our health is still far from what it could be. Why? A 1974 Canadian government report attributed all death and disease to four broad elements: inadequacies in the health care system, behavioral factors or unhealthy life-styles, environmental hazards, and human biological factors.

To be sure, there are diseases that are still beyond the control of even our advanced medical knowledge and techniques. And despite yearnings that are as old as the human race itself, there is no "fountain of youth" to ward off aging and death. Still, there is a solution to many of the problems that undermine sound health. In a word, that solution is prevention. Prevention, which includes health promotion and education, saves lives, improves the quality of life, and in the long run, saves money.

In the United States, organized public health activities and preventive medicine have a long history. Important milestones in this country or foreign breakthroughs adopted in the United States include the improvement of sanitary procedures and the development of pasteurized milk in the late 19th century and the introduction in the mid-20th century of effective vaccines against polio, measles, German measles, mumps, and other once-rampant diseases. Internationally, organized public health efforts began on a wide-scale basis with the International Sanitary Conference of 1851, to which 12 nations sent representatives. The World Health Organization, founded in 1948, continues these efforts under the aegis of the United Nations, with particular emphasis on combating communicable diseases and the training of health care workers.

Despite these accomplishments, much remains to be done in the field of prevention. For too long, we have had a medical care system that is science- and technology-based, focused, essentially, on illness and mortality. It is now patently obvious that both the social and the economic costs of such a system are becoming insupportable.

Implementing prevention—and its corollaries, health education and promotion—is the job of several groups of people.

First, the medical and scientific professions need to continue basic scientific research, and here we are making considerable progress. But increased concern with prevention will also have a decided impact on how primary care doctors practice medicine. With a shift to health-based rather than morbidity-based medicine, the role of the "new physician" will include a healthy dose of patient education.

Second, practitioners of the social and behavioral sciences—psychologists, economists, city planners—along with lawyers, business leaders, and government officials—must solve the practical and ethical dilemmas confronting us: poverty, crime, civil rights, literacy, education, employment, housing, sanitation, environmental protection, health care delivery systems, and so forth. All of these issues affect public health.

Third is the public at large. We'll consider that very important group in a moment.

Fourth, and the linchpin in this effort, is the public health profession—doctors, epidemiologists, teachers—who must harness the professional expertise of the first two groups and the common sense and cooperation of the third, the public. They must define the problems statistically and qualitatively and then help us set priorities for finding the solutions.

To a very large extent, improving those statistics is the responsibility of every individual. So let's consider more specifically what the role of the individual should be and why health education is so important to that role. First, and most obvious, individuals can protect themselves from illness and injury and thus minimize their need for professional medical care. They can eat nutritious food; get adequate exercise; avoid tobacco, alcohol, and drugs; and take prudent steps to avoid accidents. The proverbial "apple a day keeps the doctor away" is not so far from the truth, after all.

Second, individuals should actively participate in their own medical care. They should schedule regular medical and dental checkups. Should they develop an illness or injury, they should know when to treat themselves and when to seek professional help. To gain the maximum benefit from any medical treatment that they do require, individuals must become partners in that treatment. For instance, they should understand the effects and side effects of medications. I counsel young physicians that there is no such thing as too much information when talking with patients. But the corollary is the patient must know enough about the nuts and bolts of the healing process to understand what the doctor is telling him or her. That is at least partially the patient's responsibility.

Education is equally necessary for us to understand the ethical and public policy issues in health care today. Sometimes individuals will encounter these issues in making decisions about their own treatment or that of family members. Other citizens may encounter them as jurors in medical malpractice cases. But we all become involved, indirectly, when we elect our public officials, from school board members to the president. Should surrogate parenting be legal? To what extent is drug testing desirable, legal, or necessary? Should there be public funding for family planning, hospitals, various types of medical research, and other medical care for the indigent? How should we allocate scant technological resources, such as kidney dialysis and organ transplants? What is the proper role of government in protecting the rights of patients?

What are the broad goals of public health in the United States today? In 1980, the Public Health Service issued a report aptly entitled *Promoting Health—Preventing Disease: Objectives for the Nation*. This report expressed its goals in terms of mortality and in terms of intermediate goals in education and health improvement. It identified 15 major concerns: controlling high blood pressure; improving family planning; improving pregnancy care and infant health; increasing the rate of immunization; controlling sexually transmitted diseases; controlling the presence of toxic agents and radiation in the environment; improving occupational safety and health; preventing accidents; promoting water fluoridation and dental health; controlling infectious diseases; decreasing smoking; decreasing alcohol and drug abuse; improving nutrition; promoting physical fitness and exercise; and controlling stress and violent behavior.

For healthy adolescents and young adults (ages 15 to 24), the specific goal was a 20% reduction in deaths, with a special focus on motor vehicle injuries and alcohol and drug abuse. For adults (ages 25 to 64), the aim was 25% fewer deaths, with a concentration on heart attacks, strokes, and cancers.

Smoking is perhaps the best example of how individual behavior can have a direct impact on health. Today, cigarette smoking is recognized as the single most important preventable cause of death in our society. It is responsible for more cancers and more cancer deaths than any other known agent; is a prime risk factor for heart and blood vessel disease, chronic bronchitis, and emphysema; and is a frequent cause of complications in pregnancies and of babies born prematurely, underweight, or with potentially fatal respiratory and cardiovascular problems.

Since the release of the Surgeon General's first report on smoking in 1964, the proportion of adult smokers has declined substantially, from 43% in 1965 to 30.5% in 1985. Since 1965, 37 million people have quit smoking. Although there is still much work to be done if we are to become a "smoke-free society," it is heartening to note that public health and public education efforts—such as warnings on cigarette packages and bans on broadcast advertising—have already had significant effects.

In 1835, Alexis de Tocqueville, a French visitor to America, wrote, "In America the passion for physical well-being is general." Today, as then, health and fitness are front-page items. But with the greater scientific and technological resources now available to us, we are in a far stronger position to make good health care available to everyone. And with the greater technological threats to us as we approach the 21st century, the need to do so is more urgent than ever before. Comprehensive information about basic biology, preventive medicine, medical and surgical treatments, and related ethical and public policy issues can help you arm yourself with the knowledge you need to be healthy throughout your life.

FOREWORD

Dale C. Garell, M.D.

Advances in our understanding of health and disease during the 20th century have been truly remarkable. Indeed, it could be argued that modern health care is one of the greatest accomplishments in all of human history. In the early 20th century, improvements in sanitation, water treatment, and sewage disposal reduced death rates and increased longevity. Previously untreatable illnesses can now be managed with antibiotics, immunizations, and modern surgical techniques. Discoveries in the fields of immunology, genetic diagnosis, and organ transplantation are revolutionizing the prevention and treatment of disease. Modern medicine is even making inroads against cancer and heart disease, two of the leading causes of death in the United States.

Although there is much to be proud of, medicine continues to face enormous challenges. Science has vanquished diseases such as smallpox and polio, but new killers, most notably AIDS, confront us. Moreover, we now victimize ourselves with what some have called "diseases of choice," or those brought on by drug and alcohol abuse, bad eating habits, and mismanagement of the stresses and strains of contemporary life. The very technology that is doing so much to prolong life has brought with it previously unimaginable ethical dilemmas related to issues of death and dying. The rising cost of health care is a matter of central concern to us all. And violence in the form of automobile accidents, homicide, and suicide remains the major killer of young adults.

In the past, most people were content to leave health care and medical treatment in the hands of professionals. But since the 1960s, the consumer of medical care—that is, the patient—has assumed an increasingly central role in the management of his or her own health. There has also been a new emphasis placed on prevention: People are recognizing that their own actions can help prevent many of the conditions that have caused death and disease in the past. This accounts for the growing commitment to good nutrition and regular exercise, for the increasing number of people who are choosing not to smoke, and for a new moderation in people's drinking habits.

People want to know more about themselves and their own health. They are curious about their body: its anatomy, physiology, and bio-chemistry. They want to keep up with rapidly evolving medical technologies and procedures. They are willing to educate themselves about common disorders and diseases so that they can be full partners in their own health care.

THE ENCYCLOPEDIA OF HEALTH is designed to provide the basic knowledge that readers will need if they are to take significant responsibility for their own health. It is also meant to serve as a frame of reference for further study and exploration. The encyclopedia is divided into five subsections: The Healthy Body; The Life Cycle; Medical Disorders & Their Treatment; Psychological Disorders & Their Treatment; and Medical Issues. For each topic covered by the encyclopedia, we present the essential facts about the relevant biology; the symptoms, diagnosis, and treatment of common diseases and disorders; and ways in which you can prevent or reduce the severity of health problems when that is possible. The encyclopedia also projects what may lie ahead in the way of future treatment or prevention strategies.

The broad range of topics and issues covered in the encyclopedia reflects that human health encompasses physical, psychological, social, environmental, and spiritual well-being. Just as the mind and the body are inextricably linked, so, too, is the individual an integral part of the wider world that comprises his or her family, society, and environment. To discuss health in its broadest aspect it is necessary to explore the many ways in which it is connected to such fields as law, social science, public policy, economics, and even religion. And so, the encyclopedia is meant to be a bridge between science, medical technology, the world at large, and you. I hope that it will inspire you to pursue in greater depth particular areas of interest and that you will take advantage of the suggestions for further reading and the lists of resources and organizations that can provide additional information.

CHAPTER 1

WHAT IS SLEEP?

The Greek philosopher Aristotle (384–322 B.C.), a forerunner of modern sleep researchers, suggested that sleep was controlled within the body itself rather than by external forces.

Most people spend one-third of their life asleep, yet this seemingly quiet state of being has remained a constant source of mystery and conjecture through the millennia.

Prehistoric humans believed that the soul actually leaves the body during sleep, and ancient cultures later worshiped gods they believed were responsible for sleep. The Greeks called such a deity Hypnos, and the Romans named him Somnus. The goddess of night was mother to both Somnus and his brother Orcus, the god of death.

Ancient Greece was home to what was perhaps the first objective investigation of sleep. Around 350 B.C., the philosopher Aristotle looked beyond mythology to infer that sleep is a result of natural bodily functions. Based on his observations of physical occurrences during sleep, Aristotle explained that sleep involved "conservation" and "an inhibition of sense perception"—an idea far ahead of its time.

After Aristotle's efforts, a long period of time elapsed when little was learned about the subject of sleep. Referred to as the prescientific period, the era's only "experts" on sleep and dreams were poets and dream diviners.

This dark period came to a close in 1846 when Dr. Edward Binns published *The Anatomy of Sleep*. Although the book contained basically anecdotes and hearsay, it did include what little information was newly available on human physiology. This reintroduced scientific methods to the study of sleep.

From the 1870s to the 1920s, an increased knowledge of the body's biochemical processes and central nervous system brought on a period of elementary scientific exploration into sleep. With each new insight into a physiological process, researchers thought they could identify the cause of sleep. For example, as they discovered the relationship of oxygen to blood, scientists would theorize—incorrectly—how such interactions triggered sleep. Similarly, as more was learned about the nervous system, researchers suggested that nerve cells inhibit stimuli that keep the mind awake. This particular theory was a forerunner of modern research that links the brain and sleep.

In the 1930s, the invention of instruments that measure brain activity during sleep opened a whole new world of research and with it a new view of sleep itself. Although there is still much to know, scientists now recognize that sleep is not only essential but also amazingly complex.

SLEEP: THE BODY

Sleep is not oblivion. On the contrary, many events occur in the body during this state: Blood pressure falls, the heartbeat slows, muscles relax, and the body's metabolic rate decreases by about 20%.

Butterflies are among the animals that undergo alternating patterns of activity and rest, yet their rest period is not considered sleep. They do not show the complex brain-wave patterns seen in more highly developed animals during sleep.

Sleep is an active state found only in animals with highly developed brains. Butterflies rest, but they do not sleep. Humans sleep. The difference between rest and sleep lies in the brain, which controls the sleeping state. Although the function of sleep is still not completely understood, decades of research have helped scientists identify centers in the brain that both cause sleep and control a complex order of events during sleep. Though sleep passes through various stages, much of its most important activity occurs during a mysterious phase called *REM sleep*, when the sleeper unknowingly experiences *rapid eye movement*.

Brain-wave studies of animals show that only animals with highly developed brains sleep. Most animals, even worms and flies, show daily patterns of alternating activity and rest, but whether these rest periods are defined as sleep depends on each animal's brain-wave patterns. For example, the inert state of a butterfly during the night is called *dormancy* rather than sleep because no brain-wave patterns typical of sleep can be detected.

A somewhat more sleeplike condition, called *shallow torpor*, is found in some small mammals and birds. In this state, their rate of activity decreases considerably and their body temperature drops sharply. In such birds as the hummingbird, shallow torpor occurs on a daily basis, apparently as an energy-saving mechanism.

Deep torpor, or *hibernation*, occurs in a limited number of mammals, most of them small. Studies find that hibernating animals first

Contrary to popular opinion, bears do not truly hibernate because they may wake up and even walk around on mild winter days. Most hibernators are smaller mammals that conserve a great amount of energy when their body temperature drops and brain activity disappears.

fall asleep, then their body temperature drops steadily, and eventually all brain activity disappears. Hibernation helps animals avoid dying of cold: They save a great deal of energy when they no longer need to maintain a high body temperature. Like shallow torpor and sleep, hibernation is controlled by the brain, but it eventually progresses through various phases of sleep to an end of detectable brain activity.

Reptiles also sleep. Laboratory studies have examined reptiles such as turtles and chameleons during rest periods and found brain-wave patterns similar to those of human sleepers. Like humans, many reptiles exhibit rapid eye movement, but these motions are not accompanied by the brain-wave patterns seen in humans during REM sleep. No brain waves characteristic of sleep have been detected in fish, frogs, or other amphibians.

Birds sleep also. In the 1960s, French physiologist Marcel Klein made the first study of bird sleep and found that the brain-wave patterns of sleeping chickens are similar to the patterns of both deep sleep and REM sleep in humans. The chickens, however, spent a relatively short amount of time in REM sleep. A Mexican physiologist, José Rajas-

Ramirez, recorded the brain waves of sleeping falcons and found longer periods of REM sleep.

LENGTH OF SLEEP

Generally, smaller animals sleep more than larger ones. However, size is only one factor that affects an animal's amount of sleep. Safety also plays an important role in how much an animal may sleep. If an animal is a predator, it is usually safe enough to get more sleep. If it is usually preyed upon, it must remain more awake and aware. Of course, where an animal lives also affects how vulnerable it is to attack while sleeping.

A bat, a predator that lives tucked away in caves, sleeps about 20 hours a day. A shrew, a mammal about the same size as a bat, forages in the open, hardly sleeping at all. Hamsters, which are larger and have safe underground burrows, sleep a lot. Hooved animals, which are prey in the wild, do not sleep much. If they live in a herd, some will sleep while others remain awake serving as sentinels. Lions will sleep for two or three days after gorging on a kill because they have no predators to fear.

Sleep is also a way to preserve energy, because the body's metabolic rate goes down during sleep. Yet the metabolic rate during sleep decreases by only about 10%, and such differences may have little effect on an animal's amount of sleep. Smaller animals have higher metabolic rates, but sometimes they sleep less if when awake they are safer from predators.

THE FUNCTIONS OF SLEEP

Although theories abound, the function of sleep remains unknown. A 1990 National Institute of Medicine report states, "The enigma of sleep's purpose remains one of the great unsolved questions of sleep research; without a clear-cut functional role for sleep, the types of structure-mechanism-function reasoning that have been so powerful in guiding research in all other areas of physiology and behavior are not available."

Sleep deprivation studies with animals indicate that one function of sleep could be to help control body temperature. When rats are deprived of sleep for prolonged periods, their food consumption doubles, but their body weight goes down. Heat production also increases, but temperature goes down because the body loses that heat. This suggests that sleep is linked to the body's ability to control its temperature.

At least one function of sleep appears obvious: rest. Sleep is a time of renewal that helps the body meet the demands of the waking hours. Because the body's metabolic rate decreases during sleep, sleeping allows people to conserve energy. This function of sleep applies to the brain as well as to the physical body. Alertness decreases as one stays awake longer, and a good night's sleep helps a person work and study better.

Evidence supports the belief that sleep restores mental alertness. Most brain centers lower their activity during sleep, and some shut down completely. Such shutdowns are known to occur during REM sleep, especially in brain centers that are important to memory and alertness. The nerve cells of these brain centers use specific kinds of neurotransmitters, the chemicals that send signals from one nerve cell to another. A shutdown of activity during sleep allows the nerve cells to replenish their neurotransmitter supplies in order to function better during the waking hours.

Sleep and Development

Another theory of sleep function focuses on the early years of life, starting in the womb. Sleep is believed to be a time when the developing organism begins to organize brain function. Even in the womb the human fetus sleeps, and up to 80% of that sleep is REM sleep.

Studies of sleep during development focus on REM sleep, partly because babies spend more of their time in REM sleep than adults do. Another reason is that REM sleep is controlled by the brain stem, the part of the brain that develops first and then controls basic functions such as breathing and swallowing. One theory suggests that these

Educators who recommend getting a good night's sleep before an important exam are offering sound advice. Sleep is known to provide rest for both the body and the mind, improving both memory and alertness.

essential functions, including the need for sleep, are developed during fetal REM sleep.

Sleep and Learning

Sleep is also considered an important aspect of learning and memory, both early in development and throughout life. Research on learning and memory again focuses on REM sleep. Animal studies find that deprivation of REM sleep slows the learning process, and conversely, during periods of intense training, REM sleep increases. One theory based on these studies states that knowledge gathered during waking hours is stored in permanent memory during sleep by changes in brain cells, which form new connections for new memories.

However, most researchers do not believe the theory that conscious learning can take place during sleep. They think people who buy tapes and play them under their pillows at night to painlessly learn a foreign language or some other subject are wasting their money. Some celebrated discoveries have occurred during dreams—in chemistry, the circular structure of the benzene molecule was discovered by a scientist in a dream—but such insights involve integration of existing knowledge, rather than the acquisition of new knowledge. The sleeping brain does not appear capable of absorbing new information unless it is aroused—meaning it is no longer asleep. Nevertheless, many people find the minutes between wakefulness and sleep a productive period for finding answers to pending problems.

Sleep and Hormones

Hormonal changes also appear to be controlled by sleep. The *pituitary gland*, sometimes called the body's master gland, secretes a number of hormones in response to signals from a brain center called the *hypothalamus*. One part of the hypothalamus, called the *suprachiasmatic nucleus*, is the internal *biological clock* that plays a major role in deciding when a person sleeps and when hormones are secreted.

For example, the pituitary gland releases large amounts of growth hormone when the period of deep sleep begins—lending some truth to the traditional parental wisdom that a good night's sleep will help children grow. Getting the proper amount of growth hormone is especially important because a shortage of the hormone would cause dwarfism and an excess would cause giantism.

As the early adolescent years approach, sleep is the time when the pituitary releases *luteinizing hormone*, which stimulates the sexual organs to become mature. In the adult years, *prolactin*, a hormone involved in milk production in women, is released continually during sleep, whereas the release of *thyroid-stimulating hormone* (thyrotropin) is reduced. The thyroid is the gland that helps regulate the body's use of energy.

Sleep and its hormonal changes are also linked to the rhythm of day and night. These hormonal changes are among the many circadian rhythms (built-in daily patterns that determine, for example, what time an individual becomes tired and falls asleep and what time he or she wakes up) that are basic mechanisms in most living things.

SLEEP AND THE BODY

Physical Changes

Though researchers are unclear about the function of sleep, they are able to identify many changes that occur in the body during sleep. The .

electrical resistance of the skin increases. Muscles relax. Blood vessels in the skin widen, and blood temperature drops. In the respiratory system the muscles that line the pharynx, the airway leading to the lungs, relax. Because the nerves controlling the pharynx muscles become less active during sleep, the pharynx narrows, causing snoring in some people. In addition, the nerve centers that stimulate breathing when blood levels of carbon dioxide go up do not work as efficiently during sleep.

Heart function also changes during sleep, so that the heartbeat slows (less in a poor sleeper than a sound sleeper) and becomes less regular. This loss of regularity may be a factor in both heart disease in adults and *SIDS* (sudden infant death syndrome), the major cause of death for infants in the first year of life. SIDS causes apparently healthy infants to die quietly in their sleep, possibly due to a subtle abnormality of the nerve centers that control breathing. Researchers are trying to identify the changes in the respiratory and cardiac systems associated with the syndrome.

In experiments conducted by Harvey Moldofsky of Toronto Western Hospital, some aspects of the immune system appear to be enhanced during sleep. After taking blood samples from sleeping volunteers, Moldofsky found an increase in immune activity during deep sleep. The increase paralleled a rise in blood levels of interleukin-1, a chemical the body makes to stimulate certain cells of the immune system. However, sleep deprivation studies by Moldofsky found that while lack of sleep changed the pattern of immune responses, no overall loss of immune function occurred.

Sleep and Movement

Even during sleep, the body keeps moving about. Studies in the sleep laboratory of J. Allan Hobson of Harvard Medical School found that some sleepers move as few as 8 times a night and even remain still for hours, while others move as many as 30 times a night. Hobson and his colleagues created an index that compared the amount of movement with the quality of sleep reported by individuals. The people who had the best night's sleep were those who moved the least.

Sleepwalking is generally caused by an over-abundance of activity in the upper brain centers during sleep. The disorder typically affects children, who outgrow it as their brain centers develop.

This sort of limited movement is not a sleep disorder but a natural part of many people's sleep patterns. However, such movement as *sleepwalking* and *sleep talking* are classified as sleep disorders. Those problems occur when parts of the brain that should be turned off during sleep remain active.

Sleepwalking is most common during childhood, with estimates that about 20% of children aged 5 to 7 have some sleepwalking episodes, some of which are as simple as sitting up in bed. In others, the sleeper gets out of bed and engages in complex activity, walking about the house or even into the street. Closely related to sleepwalking are sleep talking, *bruxism* (grinding of the teeth), and automatic kicking, called *nocturnal myoclonus*. Whereas sleepwalking is most common in children, bruxism and myoclonus are found more frequently in older sleepers. The general explanation for these phenomena is that the upper brain centers that control certain aspects of movement and other behaviors can become activated during sleep.

A related condition, called *REM sleep behavior disorder*, usually occurs in men over the age of 50. For some unknown reason, victims of this disorder act out the movements they are dreaming about—making swimming motions (if the dream is about swimming), turning the wheel of an imaginary automobile, even jumping out of bed if the dream calls for it. The cause of this disorder is an unexplained loss of the normal ability to disconnect dream content from the command centers of the brain.

The study of these disorders and the brain activity that causes them is helping researchers understand what the brain and body undergo during sleep.

CHAPTER 2

A NIGHT'S SLEEP

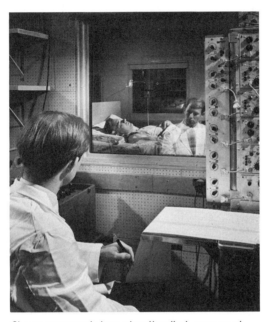

Sleep research has drastically improved since the invention of the electroenceph- alograph, an instrument that enables scientists to record brain-wave activity.

READING BRAIN WAVES

Sleep researchers define events that occur during sleep in terms of what they see on the *electroencephalograph*, an instrument that records brain waves. When researchers place sensitive electrodes on a subject's head, they pick up the signals produced by the electri- cal activity in the brain, which is then recorded as an *electroen-*

cephalogram, or EEG. An EEG offers a sort of continuing photograph of brain waves as they occur over an extended period.

An EEG diagram consists of a series of jagged, spiked waves. Each wave is described in terms of its amplitude (height) and frequency (number of waves per second). As early as the 1930s, sleep researchers began to identify characteristic wave patterns associated with different periods of sleep.

Those wave patterns are produced by electrical activity of the nerve cells, called *neurons*, that make up the brain. Neurons in the brain communicate with nerve cells in the rest of the body, transmitting and receiving information needed to perform just about every function required to sustain life. Neuron activity is partly electrical and partly chemical. When a neuron is activated, or *fired*, charged electrical particles pour into it, producing a sharp voltage. The voltage impulse carries to the end of the neuron, where it causes the release of chemicals called *neurotransmitters*. These chemicals cross the gap to the adjacent

The nerve cells, or neurons, of the brain produce electrical charges that pass from one neuron to another in a chain reaction called a brain wave.

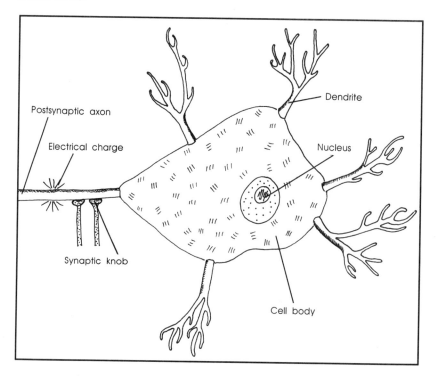

neuron, causing it to fire. The sum of these chain reactions creates an identifiable brain-wave pattern that can change in response to a change in the level of brain activity.

STAGES OF SLEEP

When a person first closes his or her eyes after getting into bed, a distinctive change in brain-wave patterns occurs. When the eyes close, the waking EEG pattern changes to show waves that are slower but have a higher amplitude. Known as *theta waves*, these brain waves define what is called stage 1 sleep—light, dozing sleep.

The next stages have distinct EEG patterns as well. Stage 2 is the first true stage of sleep, and stage 3 marks the beginning of deep sleep. Stage 4 is the deepest sleep. An EEG for a person in stage 4 sleep has more slow waves than in any other stage. In a healthy sleeper, the progression from stage 1 to stage 4 takes about one hour. After a period of stage 4 sleep, the cycle reverses itself, moving more rapidly back to stage 1 sleep. The complete cycle takes 90 to 100 minutes.

At the end of the cycle, something different is seen. The EEG record begins to show wave patterns that look more like stage 1 sleep. As mentioned previously, although the eyes remain closed, instruments detect flurries of rapid eye movement, causing this stage of sleep to be called REM sleep. The REM stage of sleep is considered the most interesting, partly because it is the period when dreams occur. Sometimes REM sleep is called *paradoxical sleep*, because the EEG indicates sleep is light even though a sleeper is actually difficult to awaken.

The type of complex brain necessary to sustain REM sleep appears rather far along the evolutionary trail in more advanced mammals. For example, humans and rats exhibit REM sleep, but the primitive egg-laying mammal known as the echidna does not. (Scientists, therefore, deduce that REM sleep originated more recently than 120 million years ago, when the first mammals, such as the echidna, evolved.)

Aside from brain-wave patterns, each stage of sleep appears to have other specific characteristics as well. During deep, slow-wave sleep in stages 3 and 4, a person has few body movements and slow, regular breathing. In contrast, during REM sleep a lot is happening in both the

Awake stage

Stage 1

Stage 2

Stage 3

Stage 4

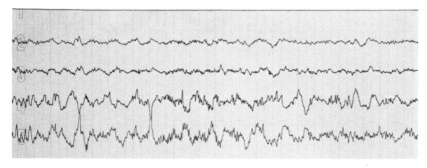

REM stage

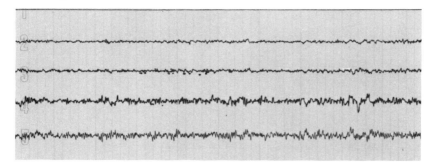

Brain-wave patterns during sleep are recorded onto an electroencephalogram (EEG), a continuing "photograph" revealing changes in the brain's electrical activity as an individual passes through various stages of sleep.

body and the brain. In addition to rapid eye movement, REM sleep contains a good deal of muscle movement: tossing and turning and activation of the brain centers that control vision and hearing. Men often have erections, and women have an increased blood flow to the genital region during REM sleep.

The cycle from stage 1 to stage 4 then to REM sleep is generally repeated 4 or 5 times in a typical night's sleep. As the night goes on, REM sleep episodes grow longer with less and less deep sleep. REM sleep usually accounts for about one quarter of the night's sleep.

In actual time, a typical night's sleep varies greatly from one person to another. Some individuals need 9 to 10 hours of sleep; others get along indefinitely on 5 or 6 hours. The average night's sleep is about seven and one-half hours. Regardless of how much time one spends in bed, one constant remains: Everyone needs REM sleep.

RHYTHMS OF SLEEP

In an important set of experiments in the 1960s, Jurgen Aschoff and Rutger Wever of the Max Planck Institute in Germany put human volunteers into special underground laboratories that offered no clues to the length of day. The volunteers spent a month in the laboratory with instructions to sleep once a day but not to nap. Their periods of sleep were recorded by a variety of instruments.

Over the 30-day period, each volunteer's sleep rhythm began to go out of phase with a 24-hour day. Most of the volunteers began to live longer days of 25 hours or more. Yet the 24-hour rhythm was restored after they left the laboratory and were exposed to the normal cycle of day and night. Obviously, the internal rhythms of sleep are not always coordinated exactly with those of night and day.

Similar experiments show that other mammals also have internal sleep-and-wake rhythms that differ from the 24-hour day. Though the cause is not clear, this strengthens the conclusion that humans sleep the way they do because of signals from their environment, despite an internal clock that runs on a slightly different schedule.

Yet there remains no such explanation for the well-known differences between "larks," the people who work best in the morning as soon

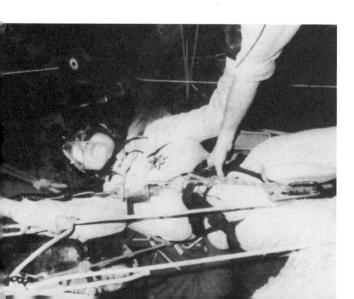

Experiments that place volunteers in isolation, with no clues as to the time of day or night, offer an important way to measure the body's natural sleep rhythms. In a 1988 study in France, Veronique le Guin emerges from an underground cavern after participating in such an experiment.

as they get up, and "owls," those who work best in the evening. Other factors, as yet unidentified, play a role in the owl-lark distinction.

THE NEED FOR SLEEP

What happens when signals from the environment are disturbed or when a person is forced to ignore them? One answer comes from studies of sleep deprivation. Volunteers who are deprived of sleep for three or four days lose concentration. They perform well on short tests but make many mistakes in long, repetitive tasks.

Longer periods of sleep deprivation result in more serious problems. (The current record for sleeplessness is held by Robert McDonald, a Californian who stayed awake for 18 days, 21 hours, and 40 minutes in 1980.) After a number of days without sleep, subjects show irritability, slurred speech, memory loss, and blurred vision. They also report hallucinations and paranoid thoughts. Yet they quickly return to normal after a long night's sleep.

Surprisingly, however, sleep deprivation experiments have caused clinically significant improvement in individuals who suffer from depression. Experiments have shown that depressed patients who are deprived specifically of REM sleep benefit the most from sleep deprivation. That benefit is limited, however, because it ends when the patient returns to regular sleep patterns. Researchers are still exploring the brain mechanisms involved in this effect.

Jet Lag

A common source of sleep disruption is jet travel. Although this has become a quick and commonplace way of getting around for millions of people, it also produces jet lag, the discomfort that occurs when a person's biological clock goes out of sequence with the time of day, so that he or she may need to sleep during daylight hours or be wide awake late at night. For example, if a person flies west to east, from New York to Europe, that individual experiences a night that is about five hours shorter than usual. It may take several days to reset the internal body

Jet lag is a well-known source of sleep disruption that results when a person's biological clock must suddenly adjust to the day-and-night light patterns of a new location.

clock to the new night-and-day schedule. Flying east to west is less disturbing, because the biological clock adjusts better to a longer day.

A few remedies have been proposed to limit jet-lag problems. The usual advice is to get up earlier and earlier in the days before a long flight from west to east. Most recently, researchers have begun to recommend immediate exposure to bright light after a long flight because it speeds resetting of the biological clock.

The Late Shift

Shift work is another practice that hinders the biological clock from staying in synchronization with day and night. Shift work, in which work schedules change periodically and require people to change their hours of sleep, is more common than most people know. According to a 1977 report by the National Institute of Occupational Safety and Health, one of four American workers is engaged in shift work. However, the unsynchronized biological clock of shift workers is more than just an inconvenience for a few. In 1988, an expert committee announced that loss of alertness during the night hours contributed to many accidents.

Some of these nighttime accidents are well known. The meltdown at the Three Mile Island nuclear generating plant in Pennsylvania occurred between 4:00 A.M. and 6:00 A.M., when operators failed to take correct action during a loss of coolant water. The nuclear accident at Chernobyl occurred in the early morning, as did the grounding of the *Exxon Valdez*, which caused one of the most destructive oil spills on record. A study of more than 6,000 single-vehicle auto accidents in Texas, New York, and Israel found the peak hours of occurrence to be between 1:00 A.M. and 4:00 A.M.

In 1983, the Philadelphia police union asked Charles Czeisler, director of the Neuroendocrinology Laboratory at Brigham and Women's Hospital in Boston, to develop a new work schedule to lessen the ill effects of shift work. With the existing schedule, police officers worked six consecutive days on one shift, had two days off, then changed to a new, earlier shift.

Czeisler found this schedule did not allow enough time for adjustment to the new shift. He devised a new program where officers kept the same shift for 18 days, with a work week of 4 or 5 days. After 11 months of Czeisler's plan, reports of poor sleep dropped by one-third and reports of fatigue dropped by more than half.

Many employers are turning to *chronobiologists*, experts in circadian rhythms, to develop programs that help workers adjust to night

One of the worst oil spills in history, the grounding of the Exxon Valdez *in Valdez, Alaska, on April 27, 1989, occurred in the early morning hours, a period of time known for its high rate of accidents. Many individuals working a late shift never get enough sleep because their body does not fully adjust to a daytime sleep schedule.*

hours and shift work. Such programs rely on what are called *zeitgebers*, external signals that help set the body's internal clock. Bright light is the most obvious zeitgeber. It has been used not only to ease jet lag but also to help shift workers adjust their internal clocks more rapidly. Exercise, social events, and proper timing of meals are techniques used to create a better environment for shift workers. Even with all these aids, some people cannot adjust to shift work because their body rhythms are too strong to be overpowered by such zeitgebers. In the 1970s, Roger Broughton of the University of Ottawa proposed that a built-in tendency creates two periods of sleep during the day-night cycle. These experiments found two natural peaks of sleepiness, one in the afternoon—between 2:00 and 5:00 P.M.—and the other in the early morning hours—between 2:00 and 7:00 A.M. Volunteers who were given no clues about the time of day and were told to sleep whenever they felt like it not only changed to the 25-hour schedule but also tended to take a short nap about 12 hours after the middle of the main period of sleep. (Studies in the 1980s by Scott Campbell and others at the Max Planck Institute confirmed Broughton's findings.)

Napping

In a study of naps, David Dinges of the University of Pennsylvania reported that they generally last more than 30 minutes and consist almost entirely of deep sleep, with very little REM sleep. Dinges also found that, after napping, people not only feel better but also perform much better on mental tests.

The day-night pattern of nap and sleep is only one aspect of the body's natural biological rhythms. Now medical researchers are studying these rhythms as influences on sickness and health. Heart attacks, for example, are most likely to occur in the morning, while asthma attacks often take place at night. These observations support the statement that sleep is not oblivion: It is linked to the biological rhythms that rule much of people's lives.

CHAPTER 3

SLEEP AND AGE

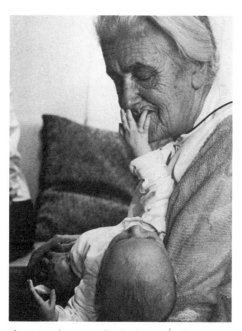

As people age, their sleep patterns evolve. A newborn baby may spend 16 out of every 24 hours asleep; most adults average 7 hours per night.

Sleep evolves continuously as people grow older. It begins in the womb and is so essential that even unborn babies experience it. A fetus's first nap begins an evolution of sleep patterns that last throughout life.

In the earliest stages of human development, even before birth, the nature of sleep depends directly on the development of the brain and nervous system. Because sleep is controlled by brain activity, one cannot sleep until his or her brain is formed. Therefore, during the early months of fetal development, when the brain and nervous system are just beginning to form, nothing resembling sleep can be detected.

Even by the 26th week of fetal development, brain activity is primitive, showing only sporadic brain waves. Before the 30th week, periods of movement by the fetus are punctuated by irregular periods of quiet, yet, according to fetal EEGs, these rest periods are not sleep. By the 32nd week, the quiet periods occur regularly, and fetal EEGs indicate that they are times of REM sleep.

BIRTH

The amount of time a fetus spends in REM sleep gradually decreases, while time spent in non-REM sleep increases, until birth at approximately 38 weeks. These changes in sleep patterns are accom-

The brain centers controlling sleep patterns begin to affect the fetus around the 30th week of development. At that point, the fetus uses REM sleep to help the brain mature further.

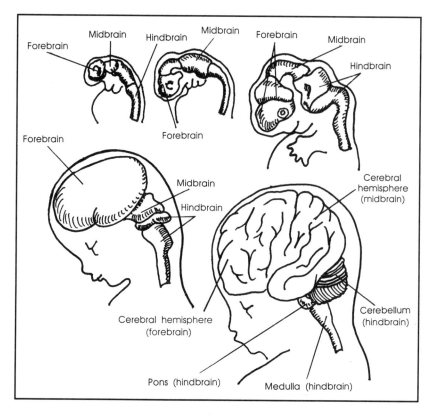

panied by an increase in the complexity of fetal EEG activity as the brain matures.

Newborn babies spend the majority of their time asleep, awakening now and then to be fed. The typical newborn will sleep 16 hours a day, spending half that time in REM sleep. For the newborn, sleep is rather disorganized at first, with the baby making no distinction between day and night. But guided by parental care and training, the infant gradually starts to sleep mostly at night, with naps during the day. Any new parent will feel relieved when the baby finally learns to sleep through the night, usually in the third or fourth month after birth.

The brain continues to develop throughout this early period of life. Various parts of the brain are still establishing connections, and the brain stem centers that control sleep are still forming. As connections are made and brain cells grow, the infant's sleep patterns change.

AN EARLY NEED FOR REM

The importance of REM sleep during early brain development has attracted special attention. Animal studies show a pattern of develop-

Between the 32nd and 36th weeks of fetal development, the amount of time the fetus spends in REM sleep already begins to decrease, while non-REM sleep increases.

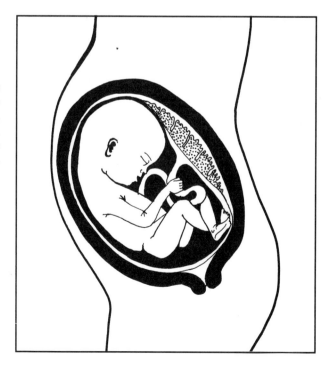

ment similar to that of humans: As in humans, a decrease in total sleep time and in REM sleep occurs in species such as the mouse, the cat, and the rabbit as they mature. Although each species differs somewhat, the similarities support the belief that REM sleep plays an important role in brain development.

In 1966 Howard Roffwarg of Columbia University proposed that the brain gets some sort of stimulation necessary for development during REM sleep. His studies, centered on the development of vision in cats, showed that during REM sleep the brain stem sends pulses of electrical signals to the brain's vision centers, which are active even when a young animal's eyes are closed. These signals carry information governing the direction and timing of eye movements during REM sleep.

CHILDHOOD

By the eighth month, an infant is awake 10 or 11 hours a day. Of the sleeping hours, about one-third are spent in REM sleep. EEGs show that the brain waves of non-REM sleep begin to take on the adult pattern at this age.

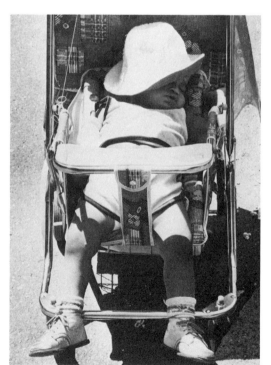

Newborns will spend half of their total sleeping time in REM sleep. Within eight months, an infant will experience REM sleep for only one-third of his or her total sleeping time. At this age, children also begin to show adult EEG sleep patterns.

During childhood, sleep behavior changes steadily toward patterns of adulthood. By age five or so, a child's disorganized periods of sleep and waking give way to a cycle of sleep at night and wakefulness at day, with an occasional daytime nap. The adult stages of sleep, ascending from stage 1 to stage 4 and back again, are also established during these years.

The transition to this adult pattern is not completely smooth. Sleep-walking is common at this age, as are other unpleasant phenomena. *Enuresis*, or bed-wetting, apparently occurs because the sleeping brain of a child has not made the connections necessary to respond to signals sent by a full bladder. Even less pleasant are *night terrors*, episodes of screaming and awakening during which the pulse pounds and blood pressure shoots up. Sometimes the child has a memory of a terrifying

By the time an individual reaches adolescence, many of his or her adult sleep patterns are firmly in place, yet teenagers typically average less than eight hours of sleep per night and their habits may be irregular. It is not unusual for an adolescent to stay up all night and then sleep late into the next day.

dream, but often he or she remembers no reason for the episode. Night terrors, enuresis, and sleepwalking, most common in childhood, occur during stages 3 and 4 of sleep.

When children enter their early school years, their amount of sleep time decreases sharply. A 5 year old sleeps 10 to 12 hours a night, perhaps with a daytime nap. An eight or nine year old sleeps about eight and one-half hours a night, usually without a nap. These older children have a lot of deep sleep in the first half of the night, with no REM sleep in the first one or two cycles. Yet even at this age, the brain is still making connections and adjustments, as many children in these years continue to experience enuresis, sleepwalking, or night terrors.

ADOLESCENCE

The amount of time spent asleep continues to decrease as a child enters adolescence. Many teenagers average less than eight hours of sleep a night, but they often sleep irregularly. A typical teenager may stay up all night or sleep well into the morning or the afternoon when given the opportunity.

The crucial event during these years is sexual maturation, which is closely involved with sleep. Teenage boys begin to have nocturnal emissions (wet dreams), sexual climaxes that happen during REM sleep. Meanwhile, the hormones responsible for sexual maturation are secreted by the pituitary gland only during non-REM sleep.

Most people experience the best sleep of their life during the middle teen years. By this time of life, the mature pattern of sleep is clearly in place, and individual patterns—lark or owl, long or short hours of sleep—have been established. Yet sleep behavior continues to evolve with age, so that the length and depth of sleep steadily decline as people grow older.

ADULTHOOD

During the early adult years the variation in individual sleep patterns emerges most clearly. A few people get by on four hours of sleep or less a night. Some require more than 10 hours. The average is eight hours a night, at least during the early adult years. People who do not sleep much appear to spend less time in stages 2 and 3 and more time in stage 4 and REM sleep.

Other individual differences in sleep patterns also emerge in a person's twenties. During these years, some people discover they prefer to stay awake late and get up late, while others find they like to go to sleep early and get up early. These are also the years when many people get married and have babies. Studies by Allan Hobson suggest that when people sleep together, their sleep becomes coordinated—they both go through the same stages of sleep, from stage 1 to REM sleep, at about the same time. The arrival of a baby obviously affects how the parents sleep, because when the baby wakes up at night, so do the parents.

A little later in life, in the late twenties or early thirties, many people begin to notice problems with sleep. Although these problems tend to increase with age, they do not necessarily affect the total amount of sleep. On the average, the length of time spent asleep does not change much in adult years, even very late in life.

AGING

Several other aspects of sleep do change with age, one of which is the number of times per night a person wakes up. Studies of volunteers by Drs. Robert Williams and Ismet Karacan showed that on the average, 75-year-old men sleep just about as much as 20-year-old men—just over 7 hours a night. Up to age 35, however, sleepers average 2 awakenings each night. By age 75, the number is 7 per night.

Individual variability in the amount of time spent asleep also becomes more noticeable with age. Younger sleepers do not vary as much from the average, while older people spend more time in bed awake. In people over 70, the average 7 hours of sleep per night covers a range from 5 to 10 hours, depending on the individual. For people under 40, waking time is less than 2% of an average night. This time increases gradually, until waking time accounts for perhaps 15% of the period that a 75-year-old spends in bed at night.

Middle age is the time when many people begin to speak wistfully about "sleeping like a baby." Sleep during middle age becomes more broken and less refreshing for a number of reasons. Many people worry more. Many have office jobs that prevent them from getting regular exercise. Many drink coffee or alcohol, both of which can interfere with sleep. But there is also a natural reason: The body spends less time in stage 4 sleep, the deepest and most restful kind. A 50-year-old who spends as much time sleeping as a 15-year-old still does not get as much refreshment from that sleep. Experts say sleep becomes more "fragile" with age.

The time at which an individual goes to sleep and wakes up also shifts with age. Older people tend to go to sleep earlier and get up earlier. This seems more a result of physical factors than of changes in a person's life-style, because a similar alteration in activity patterns is seen in studies of animals. For example, studies of nocturnal rodents, which sleep during the day and become active at night, find the older adults awake more during the day than younger ones.

On average, older people tend to spend as much time asleep as do younger adults: 75-year-old men sleep the same number of hours per night as do 20-year-old men—about 7 hours. However, many older people frequently awaken during the night or suffer from a less peaceful sleep, sometimes because of medical or social concerns.

Such research strongly suggests a change in the specific area of the brain that controls the sleep-waking cycle. Animal studies indicate that the function of this center gradually weakens with age, reducing the synchronization of the natural light-dark cycle of day and night with a person's internal sleep-wake cycle. Studies of humans also show that older workers have a harder time adjusting to rotating work shift schedules.

Sleep Difficulties Among the Aged

Just as the substantial increase of sex hormones during puberty has a major effect on sleep, their decrease later in life also takes its toll. A decline in sex hormone production, which occurs dramatically in women during menopause and more gradually in men, affects sleep negatively by making it less restful.

Older people have a greater tendency to nod off during the day. Curiously, the same kind of sleepiness overtakes many young people during the afternoon. The difference is that young people feel sleepy during the day even when they have a good night's sleep. In older people, the fragmented, broken nature of nighttime sleep often contributes to daytime drowsiness.

In the later years, retirement from active work also adds a negative effect, because it reduces levels of activity in relation to sleep. People sleep better when they are physically tired, so someone who sits around most of the day, perhaps napping too, typically has more trouble sleeping at night than a person whose days are filled with activity.

For all these and more reasons, complaints about sleep disorders are most common among older people. In a National Institute of Mental Health survey conducted in the early 1980s of nearly 8,000 Americans, 20% of those 65 and older complained of insomnia and 2% complained of *hypersomnia*, excessive sleep. Many factors add to the probability of sleep problems in older people: the death of a loved one, the tendency to take medications that interfere with sleep, and the increased physical disorders that disturb sleep.

Sleep problems are a major medical issue for senior citizens. In a study of 1,855 older people during the 1980s, Dr. Charles Pollak of Cornell Medical Center found that "in males, insomnia was the strongest predictor of both mortality and nursing home placement."

Yet old age itself is not the cause of sleep difficulties. According to a recent statement by a panel of experts from the National Institutes of Health, older people who are healthy tend not to have such difficulties.

CHAPTER 4

SLEEP RESEARCH: THE BRAIN

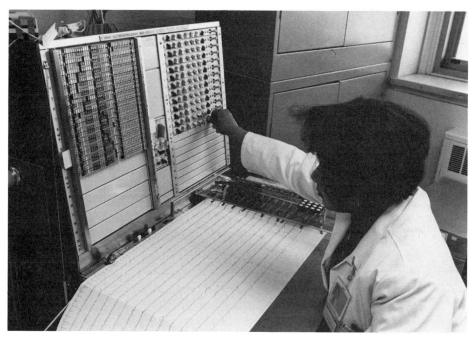

Brain research was greatly advanced by the invention of the electro-encephalograph in 1929. This device enables scientists to specify which parts of the brain are activated during each phase of sleep. Different areas of the brain offer clues to the various functions of sleep.

The golden age of sleep research has arrived. More has been learned about sleep in the last 30 years than in all of previous history. Researchers today use a great variety of instruments and techniques to concentrate their studies on the electrical and chemical activity of the brain, where sleep originates.

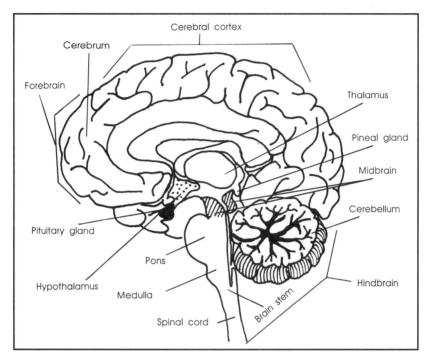

Among the brain's three primary structures—the forebrain, the midbrain, and the hindbrain—most sleep functions occur in the cerebrum of the forebrain and in the brain stem of the hindbrain.

THE BRAIN

The fact that the brain controls sleep was generally accepted early in the 19th century. Yet people still believed sleep is a time of inactivity, a period during which the brain switches itself off. Research around the turn of the century pointed toward one part of the brain as the location of the centers that turns off brain activity: the brain stem.

The brain stem is the lowest part of the brain and is attached to the spinal cord. It serves as a switchboard, making connections between the higher centers of the brain and the motor nerves that carry out their instructions. It also controls the body's basic activities, such as breathing and regulating blood pressure. The brain stem consists of several structures: the *medulla* (or *medulla oblongata*), the *reticular formation*, and the *pons*.

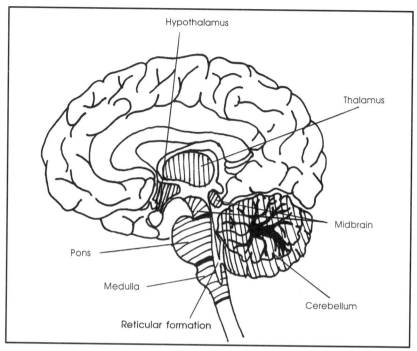

Hypothalamus

Thalamus

Midbrain

Pons

Medulla

Cerebellum

Reticular formation

During sleep the brain stem "turns off" some areas of the brain that are active during waking hours. Nevertheless, a new set of responses are turned on. The reticular formation, for example, maintains sleep by monitoring which external messages get through to the sleeping brain.

The earliest research on the brain stem occurred toward the end of World War I, when a great influenza epidemic swept the world, killing perhaps 50 million people. A number of the survivors who suffered brain damage from the infection were studied by a neurologist named Constantin Von Economo in Vienna. He discovered that those patients who suffered damage to the front of the midbrain experienced constant activity and insomnia. Those who were injured in the back of the midbrain felt lethargic and excessively sleepy. Von Economo proposed that the midbrain helps control sleep and contains two centers, one for wakefulness and one for sleep. Von Economo's theory was the first to suggest that sleep involves brain activity, rather than inactivity.

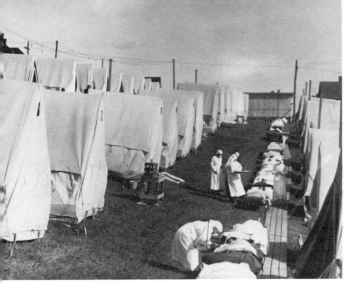

A tragic influenza epidemic killed 50 million people during the World War I era. The misfortune aided sleep research by allowing neurologists to study the sleep patterns of people who had suffered damage to specific sections of the brain.

MEASURING BRAIN WAVES

A closer look at brain-wave activity became possible with the invention of the electroencephalograph by Hans Berger, a German psychiatrist, in 1929. Berger's demonstration that brain waves could be detected by placing electrodes on the scalp called attention to the electrical activity of the brain during wakefulness and sleep. The first EEGs recorded brain waves by moving paper underneath a pen. This method was good enough to record the change from the fast, low-voltage waves of wakefulness to the slower, higher-voltage waves of drowsiness and sleep, but it could not record the brain waves' finer details.

In 1930, that deficiency was overcome by the development of the *oscilloscope*, the ancestor of today's television tube. As a pen writes with ink on paper, an oscilloscope "writes" with a beam of electrons on a *cathode-ray tube*. Its great advantage is the ability to record changes that occur in a thousandth of a second, rather than in the tenths of seconds taken by pen and paper. Researchers could finally record the EEG patterns of sleep in much greater detail.

MEASURING EYE MOVEMENTS

The next great advance in sleep research was made in 1953 in the laboratory of Nathaniel Kleitman of the University of Chicago. Eugene

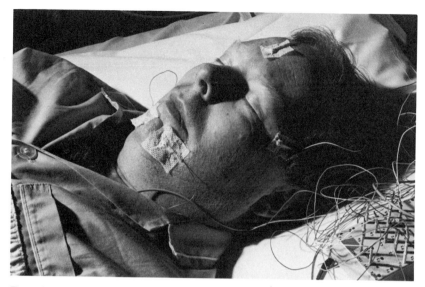

The electrooculograph (EOG), a device invented in 1953 to measure rapid eye movements during sleep, made way for the important discovery that dreams are linked to REM sleep.

Aserinsky, one of Kleitman's colleagues, studied the eye movements of children to measure how attentive they were to their surroundings while they were awake and as they fell asleep. In addition to recording the EEGs of the children, Aserinsky used an instrument called an *electrooculograph*, or EOG, to pick up the electrical signals generated by eye movements.

Aserinsky found the children had periods of rapid eye movement early in their sleep. Those periods were also times when the EEG showed low-voltage, fast brain waves somewhat similar to those seen during waking hours. In addition, Aserinsky found that this period of fast brain waves was associated with a faster pulse rate, faster breathing, and rapid eye movement. He had discovered the REM stage of sleep.

When Aserinsky did the same EEG and EOG measurements on sleeping adults, the same REM sleep patterns appeared, but during a different phase of sleep. (Children go through REM sleep as soon as they fall asleep, whereas adults experience REM sleep about 90 minutes into the sleep cycle.) Volunteers who were awakened during REM sleep spoke about their interrupted dreams—the first evidence linking this active period of sleep to dreams. The discovery of REM sleep and its connection to dreams opened up a new era in sleep research.

BRAIN MECHANISMS

Meanwhile, other researchers pursued studies of the brain mechanisms behind sleep. Their experiments indicated, for example, that the brain stem was the crucial location of the centers that generate sleep and wakefulness. Moreover, as early as the 1930s, a Belgian physiologist, Frederic Bremer, used experiments with cats to show that the forebrain—which includes the cerebral hemispheres, the higher centers of thought—produces EEG patterns of sleep. Cats whose forebrains were severed surgically fell asleep and could be aroused only by odors.

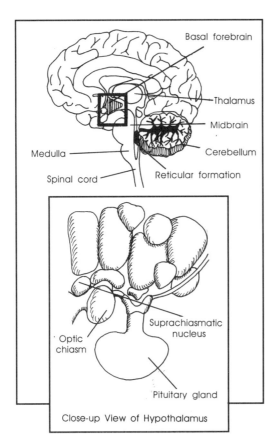

Basal forebrain

Thalamus

Midbrain

Cerebellum

Medulla

Reticular formation

Spinal cord

Suprachiasmatic nucleus

Optic chiasm

Pituitary gland

Close-up View of Hypothalamus

The brain center responsible for the sleep-wake cycle is the hypothalamus. The cycle is often referred to as a circadian rhythm, part of the body's built-in clock that keeps the body running in sync with the 24-hour day. The suprachiasmatic nucleus is now thought to be the specific area where this process occurs.

In the 1940s, Walter Hess, a Swiss physiologist, showed that wide-awake animals could be put to sleep by electrical stimulation of the *thalamus*, which is located in the central region of the brain.

At about the same time, Horace Magoun and Giuseppe Moruzzi of Northwestern University showed that sleeping animals could be awakened by electrical stimulation of a specific part of the midbrain, the reticular formation, a web of nerve cells that fans out to make contact with many brain centers.

The Sleep-Wake Cycle

At Johns Hopkins University, Curt Richter used rats running on wheels to locate the brain center responsible for the sleep-wake cycle. Although rats ordinarily are active only at night, this circadian pattern is eliminated by damage to the hypothalamus (located just above the brain stem in the midbrain). Another researcher, Robert Moore at the University of Chicago, pinpointed the exact region in the hypothalamus that apparently controls the sleep-wake cycle. It is called the suprachiasmatic nucleus.

The suprachiasmatic nucleus appears to be the brain's natural clock, processing sensory signals from the outside world to keep the body synchronized with a 24-hour day. (Without such signals, people gradually shift to a 25-hour cycle.) The suprachiasmatic nucleus sends messages to the pons, the part of the brain stem with centers that control REM and non-REM sleep.

Several other researchers support the theories on the suprachiasmatic nucleus's role in the sleep-wake cycle. At the Mitsubishi Institute in Tokyo, for example, Shin Ishi Inoue and Charles Kawamura showed that activity of suprachiasmatic nucleus cells increases and decreases on a day-to-night rhythm. Destruction of this center in animals eliminates the ordinary cycle of sleep and waking linked to day and night.

Sleep Chemicals

Constantin Von Economo, who originated sleep-related research on the brain stem toward the end of World War I, also suggested that brain centers governed waking and sleep by sending chemical signals. At that time, Parisian psychologist Henri Pieron already had evidence that such signals exist. He took spinal fluid from dogs that were kept awake for prolonged periods and injected it into dogs that were fully awake. Those animals then became sleepy. However, chemical theories were soon overshadowed by the invention of the electroencephalograph, which led scientists to concentrate on measuring brain waves.

In recent years a number of researchers have rekindled interest in Henri Pieron's work on sleep chemicals. Yet the chemistry of sleep is complex. "There is neither one sleep center nor just one sleep substance," wrote Dr. Jim Horne, director of the Sleep Research Laboratory at Loughborough University in England. "Most of the evidence so far suggests that putative sleep substances are not confined to sleep centers but are diffused through the brain."

In the early 1980s, John Pappenheimer led a research group at Harvard University that isolated a substance called *factor S* from the cerebrospinal fluid of goats who were deprived of sleep. (Cerebro-spinal fluid saturates the brain and spinal cord.) They also isolated tiny amounts of factor S from the urine of human volunteers: 3,000 quarts of urine yielded just 7 millionths of a gram of factor S. When a small fraction of this amount was injected into a rabbit, the animal slept for as long as six hours, mostly in deep non-REM sleep.

James Krueger of the University of Tennessee has since shown that factor S is a chemical, called *muramyl peptide*, similar to compounds found in the cell walls of bacteria. At first factor S was assumed to be a contaminant produced by the breakdown of bacteria in the spinal fluid. Now it is thought that muramyl peptide is not a contaminant, but a product of white blood cells after they destroy and digest bacteria. The body somehow makes use of this substance in sleep.

Krueger also demonstrated that a close relative of muramyl pep-tide, *muramyl dipeptide* (MDP), also appears to be a sleep substance. Injected into animals, MDP causes larger-than-usual amounts of non-REM sleep. MDP also raises body temperature and stimulates the immune system into action. Interestingly, sleepiness and fever are also common effects of infections, which are also known to stimulate immune system activity. MDP is believed to play an indirect part in all those responses.

Experiments by Krueger indicate that MDP acts by stimulating production of *cytokines*, infection-fighting compounds made by cells of the immune system and certain brain cells. Interleukin-1 and type II interferon are examples of cytokines that induce sleep. Although researchers do not know precisely how they work, cytokines do stimulate the activity of another naturally occurring substance, prostaglandin D_2, which enhances sleep.

Such research shows that sleep, infection, fever, and immune system activity are somehow related. However, when animals are injected with MDP and given drugs to prevent fever, the animals still become sleepy, indicating that the fever is not what causes sleepiness. Rather, the MDP acting through interleukin-1 and type II interferon creates sleepiness. Additionally, stringent exercise raises interleukin-1 blood levels, which may explain why people feel sleepy after a bout of exercise.

Another sleep substance, isolated from the blood of rabbits in the 1960s by Marcel Monnier and other researchers at the University of Basel in Switzerland, is called *delta sleep-inducing peptide* (DSIP). (A peptide is a small protein.) DSIP injections cause animals to fall quickly into deep, non-REM sleep but also increases their total amount of REM sleep. Experiments with a laboratory-made version of DSIP on human volunteers have not produced clear-cut results, perhaps because the synthetic version may differ in some way from the natural substance.

In Japan, Shojiro Inoue of the Tokyo Medical and Dental School has isolated *sleep-promoting substance* (SPS) from rats. SPS, a mixture of four compounds, makes animals sleep longer, particularly by increasing the amount of REM sleep.

The precise role of these sleep substances in the normal regulation of sleep and wakefulness still is not established. Presently, they are important as research tools, enabling scientists to induce sleep in animals at any time. For example, sleep substances help determine the effect of circadian rhythms on sleep by inducing sleep at a time of day when animals are normally awake. They also introduce powerful new methods of molecular biology into sleep research.

Once the molecular structure of a sleep substance is known, researchers try to determine where, when, and how they are produced in the brain. Molecular probes examine the mechanisms that turn sleep substances on and off during the sleep-wake cycle. Although these studies are just beginning, they promise to open up new frontiers in sleep research.

Neurotransmitters

Another aspect of brain chemistry and sleep concerns neurotransmitters, the molecules that transmit signals between nerve cells. Two

Neurotransmitters are molecules that carry signals between nerve cells. Serotonin is the neurotransmitter in the brain thought to affect states of alertness and sleepiness.

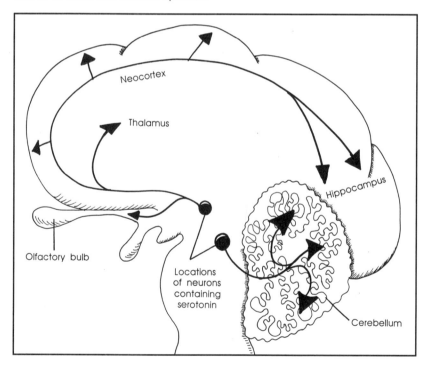

neurotransmitters that appear to play major roles in the brain's sleep centers are *serotonin* and *norepinephrine*. Serotonin has attracted the most attention in recent years because of research indicating that its concentration in the brain can affect a person's state of alertness or sleepiness. Because serotonin is acquired through certain foods, it is possible that tiredness and wakefulness may be affected by people's eating habits.

Research by Joseph and Judith Wurtman at the Massachusetts Institute of Technology established that brain levels of serotonin are affected by consumption of a substance called *L-tryptophan*. The Wurtmans' work indicates that an increase in blood levels of L-tryptophan increases production of serotonin in the brain. Since research links serotonin with sleep, this work led to the popularity of L-tryptophan as an all-natural, harmless cure for insomnia. L-tryptophan is also found abundantly in lecithin, a chemical found in foods such as egg yolk and vegetable oil and used to process foods such as margarine and chocolate.

The scientific validity of the effectiveness of L-tryptophan on insomnia is not firmly established, yet it sold widely in health food stores until 1990. At that time, all L-tryptophan was taken off the market. Laboratory studies discovered that a previously unknown

L-tryptophan, a substance found in serotonin, is thought to induce sleep. Many people make a point of consuming foods, such as milk, that contain this substance. Yet these foods probably do not contain enough of the substance to have any effect.

contaminant was found in batches of L-tryptophan sold by one Japanese manufacturer.

The contaminant led to several cases of a previously rare condition called *eosinophilia-myalgia syndrome*, which causes aching muscles and can even be fatal. The condition gets its name because its victims have reduced levels of white blood cells called *eosinophils*; myalgia is the medical name for aching muscles. Although research established a strong link between the contaminated L-tryptophan and eosinophilia-myalgia syndrome, researchers continue to investigate other effects of L-tryptophan.

CHAPTER 5

REM SLEEP RESEARCH

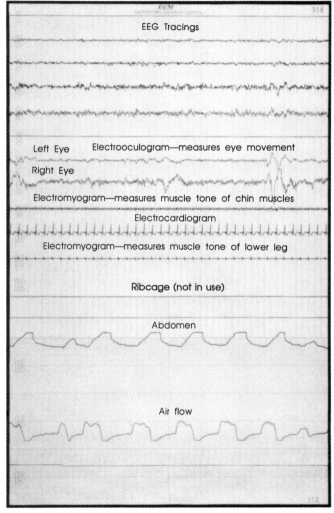

EEG Tracings

Left Eye   Electrooculogram—measures eye movement

Right Eye

Electromyogram—measures muscle tone of chin muscles

Electrocardiogram

Electromyogram—measures muscle tone of lower leg

Ribcage (not in use)

Abdomen

Air flow

Machines that electrically record the body's activities during sleep measure much more than brain waves and rapid eye movements. This reading during REM sleep also indicates movements of the chin, heart, legs, rib cage, abdomen, and air flow into the lungs.

Sleep research thrived with the recording of brain waves, a method that helped define the stages of sleep in terms of changes in brain-wave activity. Yet valuable as they are, the brain waves recorded on an EEG have definite limitations as an information source; they represent the summed activity of many millions of brain cells. Through work with animals and humans, however, scientists have begun to connect the brain waves of an EEG with the interrelated activities of the many brain centers that control sleep.

THE CORTEX

Scientists now know that in order for a person to fall asleep, signals sent from his or her brain stem must alter activity in the midbrain and the *cerebral cortex* (the layer of folded gray matter containing most of the brain's nerve cells). When people are awake, for example, the cortex constantly receives messages generated by sounds, sights, and other sensory inputs from the outside world. They are processed by the thalamus before going to the cortex.

When a person lies down in bed, turns off the light, and closes his or her eyes, he or she signals the brain to stop its constant monitoring of outside stimuli. The activity of the nerves connecting the thalamus and cortex decreases, and the individual falls into stage 2 sleep. Even so, the brain continues to monitor the environment during sleep, allowing people to respond to emergencies; a mother wakes up when her baby cries, and the smell of smoke arouses someone from deep sleep.

REM MECHANISMS

About an hour after people fall into deep sleep, some brain centers become active again, signaling the start of the REM stage. As a result, certain motor nerves go into action, not only producing eye movements and twitches but also causing an individual to dream.

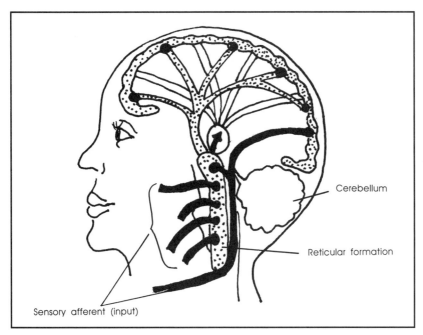

Cerebellum

Reticular formation

Sensory afferent (input)

Because people are faced with a constant flow of new information, a section of the brain called the thalamus is responsible for monitoring useful information before it reaches the cortex, which then acts on it. During wakefulness the thalamus allows a great deal of information to enter the cortex, but during sleep it permits only urgent information to alert the brain.

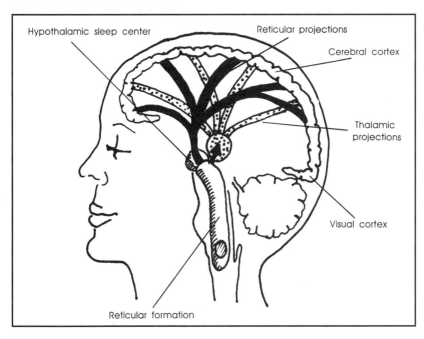

Hypothalamic sleep center

Reticular projections

Cerebral cortex

Thalamic projections

Visual cortex

Reticular formation

REM Neurotransmitters

Many detailed research projects are under way to pinpoint the brain centers and neurotransmitters involved in REM and non-REM sleep. For instance, research finds that the pons is responsible for the rapid eye movement of REM sleep. Scientists have also discovered that the nerve cells in the pons that control the REM stage use a neurotransmitter called *acetylcholine*. In animal studies, REM sleep can be induced by injecting the pons with a variety of compounds that mimic acetylcholine. A similar result is obtained in human studies by giving volunteers a drug called *physostigmine* (which also acts much like acetylcholine). When awakened from sleep, they report the same kinds

The section of the brain controlling the rapid eye movements of REM sleep is called the pons; the pons creates these movements with the help of a neurotransmitter called acetylcholine.

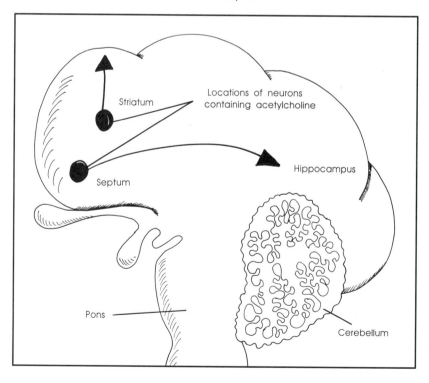

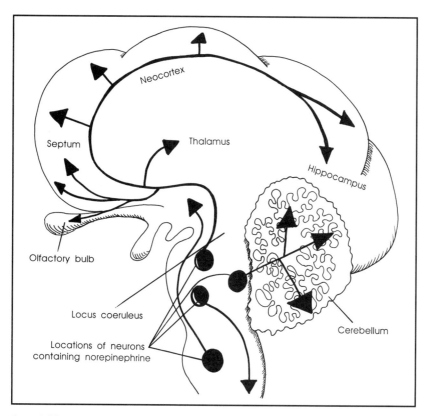

In addition to controlling rapid eye movements, the pons governs other muscle activity in the body during REM sleep using a neurotransmitter called norepinephrine.

of dreams experienced during normal REM sleep. Other studies show that drugs that block acetylcholine inhibit REM sleep in animals and humans.

In addition, research with cats has led to the discovery of a region of the brain responsible for the loss of muscle tone during REM sleep. The neurotransmitter utilized by this area is called *norepinephrine*. When the region is destroyed, cats walk about and engage in complex behavior during REM sleep. A similar sleep ailment in humans, *REM sleep behavior disorder*, also causes such activity. While asleep, a person with this disorder can perform various activities that he or she dreams about—for example, running across the room while dreaming about dashing for a commuter train.

Through these studies, researchers can try to develop treatments for different sleep problems, including *narcolepsy*, a condition that causes people to nod off at inappropriate times. Brain research shows that animals suffering from symptoms of narcolepsy can be helped by administration of neurotransmitters, especially acetylcholine and norepinephrine. As research continues, more methods may become available to help people experience healthier sleep. (For more on sleep disorders, see Chapters 7 and 8.)

CHAPTER 6

DREAMS

"To sleep, perchance to dream . . ." is the famous quote from Hamlet *that describes both the mystery surrounding dreams and the pervasive feeling that people have no control over their slumber.*

Throughout history, human beings have tried to understand their dreams. The earliest theory, one that many people still believe, is that dreams forecast coming events. The idea that dreams are messages about the future is thousands of years old. In the Old Testament, for instance, Joseph wins favor with the Egyptian Pharaoh by interpreting a dream that seven years of plenty would be followed by seven years of famine.

Sigmund Freud (1856–1939), the founder of psychoanalysis, introduced the idea that dreams express the mind's unconscious wishes in his book The Interpretation of Dreams.

A papyrus from ancient Egypt includes the belief: "If a woman kisses her husband [in a dream], she will have trouble." In classical Greece and Rome, oracles devoted much of their time to the interpretation of dreams. Even today, books that give guidance based on dreams are widely sold.

FREUDIAN THEORY OF DREAMS

The modern era of dream interpretation began in 1900, when Sigmund Freud described dreams as the mind's way of expressing unconscious wishes. Freud made dreams an integral part of his psychoanalytic theory, which maintains that unconscious primal instinct, the *id*, is kept under control by conscious higher human thought processes, or the *ego*. According to Freud, during sleep the ego slackens its vigilance, and suppressed thoughts or wishes escape from the id in the form of dreams.

In his book *The Interpretation of Dreams* Freud describes dreams as the "royal road" to unconscious thought. Dreams express warped and twisted versions of unconscious instincts, he says, but they can be analyzed to reveal the underlying aspects of people's thoughts that they prefer to keep hidden. Dream analysis by a therapist based on a patient's free association remains a central element of psychoanalysis today.

Freud's dream theory was and is controversial. Initially, conventional thinkers opposed it because they could not believe Freud's theories that sexual fantasies play such a large role in the human mind. Today, Freudian dream theory is questioned for another reason: It ignores completely the neurological mechanisms of the brain.

DREAMS AND REM SLEEP

Freud's theory was proposed long before the keystone discovery that dreams occur during REM sleep. Today, dream theories focus primarily on the neurological events that occur during the REM stage and include detailed studies of animals as well as humans (although there is no clear evidence that animals dream).

Activation-Synthesis Theory

In the early 1960s, research by William Dement at the University of Chicago showed that the brain stem sends pulsed signals to the visual center of the cortex during REM sleep. This helped J. Allan Hobson and Robert McCarley of Harvard Medical School to propose the *activation-synthesis* theory of dreams in 1977. According to Hobson, "Dreaming is the subjective awareness of brain activation in sleep," meaning that dreams consist of memories and associations that arise in the cortex in response to brain stem signals during REM sleep.

The theory says that these brain stem signals are basically the same as those sent to the cortex during waking hours. Waking signals from the brain stem usually are responses to stimuli from the outside world, and they initiate physical activity. Yet when the same signals bombard the cortex during sleep, the pathways that take in sensory signals from the outside world and put the body into motion are blocked. Therefore, signals from the brain stem do not result in physical activity. Dreams, the Hobson-McCarley theory says, are the best response the cortex can make to these signals.

The original version of the activation-synthesis theory proposed that dreams are meaningless, but Hobson and McCarley later revised their ideas to give dreams some significance. The newer theory says the sleeping brain can impose some order on random signals transmitted during sleep, and that order depends on the contents of the individual mind. Thus, dreams would offer insight into the sorts of memories and emotions residing in a person's brain. An aviator is likely to dream of airplanes, while a gardener is likely to dream of flowers.

Neural Garbage Collection

A different theory was proposed in 1983 by Francis Crick of the Salk Institute in La Jolla, California, and Graeme Mitchison of Cambridge University in England. Like Hobson and McCarley, they assumed that dreams arise when the cortex receives signals from the brain stem during sleep. They added, however, that these signals serve to activate a sort of neural "garbage collection" that disposes of unwanted information.

The brain receives an almost infinite amount of sensory data during the course of an ordinary day, Crick and Mitchison said. If the brain attempted to store all this information, the effort might overload the cortex. Dreams are the brain's way of preventing this problem, the theory suggests, comparing the signals sent from the brain stem to the cortex to strokes of an eraser; the signals methodically wipe unneeded memories from the cortex. After a dream certain memories are released from storage. Crick and Mitchison revised their theory a few years later, saying that this forgetting function applied only to more bizarre thoughts expressed in dreams and not to coherent narratives occurring in many dreams. They added a portion of Freudian theory, claiming that some of the memories erased during dreaming are connected to unwanted fantasies or obsessions.

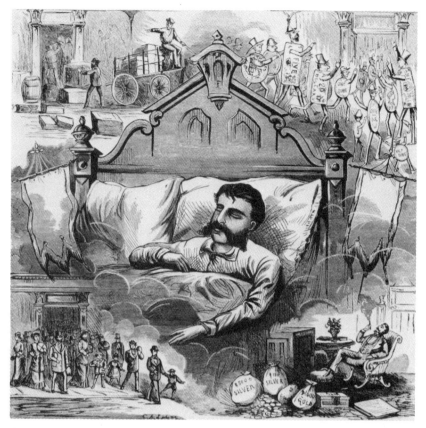

Research suggests that the brain requires a certain amount of dream time as a mental escape valve. One experiment showed that people who were deprived of their normal amount of REM sleep at night found themselves fantasizing more often during the day.

REM as an Escape Valve

In an experiment performed by a Pennsylvania researcher, Dr. Anthony Kales, volunteers were deprived of REM sleep during the first half of the night. As a result, when they slept without interruption during the second half of the night, some of them increased their normal amount of REM sleep and found themselves fantasizing during the day, some-

LUCID DREAMING

The secret world of dreams has mystified people across the ages, yet new inroads into understanding dreams have begun to appear within the past few decades. Leading this exploration are sleep researchers who have incorporated a phenomenon known as *lucid dreaming* into their work. This unusual dream state occurs—as most dreams do—during REM sleep. But the factor that makes lucid dreams different from typical dreams is consciousness: The dreamer becomes aware that he or she is dreaming while still in the dream. Upon awakening, lucid dreamers describe their dreams as vividly detailed and colorful, often accompanied by a feeling of exhilaration.

The scientific study of dreams has been hampered by the difficulty of creating and remembering normal dreams. Yet lucid dreamers allow scientists to research dreams by observing subjects who are both aware of their dreams and in control of their content. The foremost researcher of lucid dreams, Stephen La-Berge, Ph.D. of Stanford University Sleep Research Center, first demonstrated his theories on the subject in 1978 when he went into the sleep laboratory himself. Knowing that the eyes are the only part of the body that moves during REM sleep, LaBerge used eye movements to signal his initials in Morse code when he began to lucid dream. This proved that he was conscious of his dream state, while his EEG brain waves clearly showed that he was asleep. Numerous lucid dreamers have since produced a variety of evidence that has gained the scientific community's support for lucid dream research.

Once an experienced lucid dreamer realizes that he or she is dreaming, that individual can choose what to do next in the dream. In sleep lab experiments that monitor lucid dreamers, a number of subjects used eye movements to signal when they began to perform certain tasks, such as singing, counting, or holding their breath. In this way, scientists have compared the actions performed in a dream to those performed when awake and found that the bodily responses are similar. For example, when dreamers hold their breath and count the passing of five seconds, monitors show that respiration is, indeed, suspended for five seconds, just as it is if the task is performed when awake.

Lucid dreams may also serve everyday purposes. A child who suffers from nightmares can be taught to realize that he or she is dreaming and then face up to and control the fear. Additionally, a lucid dreamer may use dreams to recall past experiences and explore new possibilities in order to resolve a particular problem. LaBerge also suggests that positive feelings typically produced during lucid dreams will carry over into the waking state.

In his book *Lucid Dreaming*, LaBerge describes a technique that he believes most people can use to induce lucid dreams on a fairly consistent basis. Called Mnemonic Induction of Lucid Dreams (MILD), it recommends:

1. When awakening from a dream, review it several times until it is memorized.

2. While still in bed say, "The next time I dream I want to remember to recognize I'm dreaming."

3. Picture being back in the dream, yet realizing that it is a dream.

4. Repeat the second and third steps until falling back to sleep.

LaBerge stresses that the most important component of this technique is *intention*: The dreamer must be confident that he or she will dream. To develop this confidence, many dreamers must first learn to recognize that they are experiencing a dream. This is achieved by noticing clues to the dreamlike nature of an experience, such as unusual inconsistencies or a memory of similar events having occurred in previous dreams. To be assured that one is indeed dreaming, a lucid dreamer can perform an action that would be impossible when awake, such as flying.

For the individual who wants to dream more often, LaBerge offers practical advice: Sleep more. As the night's sleep cycle progresses, stages of REM sleep occur more frequently and last longer, while stages 3 and 4 (the deepest phases of non-active sleep) decrease. Thus, when a person sleeps 7 hours, 50% of his or her dreams occur in the last 2 hours—whereas, when he or she sleeps 1 extra hour, most of that time contains dreams. This also helps a person remember dreams, and many serious dreamers use this opportunity to record their dream experiences upon awakening.

thing they did not typically do. Other volunteers, who normally fantasized during the day, had no increase in REM sleep during the second half of the night and no more day fantasies than usual. These findings suggest that the brain requires a quota of dreams or fantasies as an escape valve and that REM sleep is a normal means of relief.

DREAM RESEARCH

Dream research is the most likely way to settle the debate concerning the purpose of dreams. Several approaches are possible. One technique is to awaken sleepers during REM sleep and ask them to recall their dreams. A second method is to study the brain mechanisms of REM sleep in animals and humans. By putting information from both approaches together, researchers can try to establish the reasons behind dreams.

Allan Hobson and his collaborators at Harvard University use a device called the *Nightcap* to help them conduct investigations. It consists of an ordinary tennis headband modified to carry sensors that record eye and body movement during sleep. (Deep sleep is defined as an absence of body and eye motion; REM sleep as eye motion with no body motion.) While sophisticated EEG recording equipment must be used in a sleep laboratory, the Nightcap is simple enough to use in an ordinary bedroom to record the stages of sleep. Hobson has used both the Nightcap and EEGs to record hundreds of dream brain-wave patterns.

A different approach was used in the 1970s by Howard Roffwarg and colleagues at Columbia University in research relating the direction of rapid eye movement to the content of dreams. Roffwarg's work is summed up by the "scanning theory" of dreaming, which says that the direction of eye movements is the key element in dream content. He suggested, for example, that if someone dreams of going upstairs, the eye movements are up and down; if someone dreams of playing ping-pong, the movements are side to side. Similar experiments have, however, failed to produce supporting evidence, causing the scanning theory to lose popularity recently.

THETA RHYTHM

A dream theory proposed by Jonathan Winson at the Rockefeller University in New York City focuses on one specific component of brain activity: *theta rhythm*, a brain wave of about six cycles per second seen during waking hours and REM sleep in a number of animals. (Theta rhythm is so named because it has the same frequency as the theta waves seen on EEGs.) Unlike theta waves, theta rhythms are not seen in humans, monkeys, and other primates. However, studying theta rhythm may offer insight into the evolution of REM sleep.

Experiments by Winson and others have led him to suggest that theta rhythm is generated during behaviors that are crucial to the survival of a species. Theta rhythm appears in rabbits when they are being hunted, in cats when they are hunting, and in rats when they are exploring strange territory. Theta rhythm, Winson proposed, is the brain's way of assimilating important new information and adding it to memory. Thus, the presence of theta rhythm during REM sleep in many animals indicates that this process of memory assimilation and storage is occurring at the time and that dreams play a central role in the process.

In other words, Winson believes that REM sleep is the period when information gathered during the day ". . . may be accessed again and integrated with past experience to provide an ongoing strategy for

An echidna, or spiny anteater; the echidna, the oldest existing type of mammal, does not undergo REM sleep. This fact indicates that REM sleep and its functions developed in mammals sometime after the echidna first appeared 120 million years ago.

behavior. . . . Dreaming may reflect a memory-processing mechanism inherited from lower species, in which information important for survival is reprocessed during REM sleep."

A baby's constant need for REM sleep supports the theory that mammals use REM sleep as a time to absorb and integrate information from the outside world during the early stages of life.

Winson uses the echidna to support his theory. Although this primitive mammal does not experience REM sleep, it does possess a very large cortex—bigger (in relation to the rest of the brain) than any other mammal's—for processing memory, Winson maintains. The cortex in higher mammals is smaller but more efficient, he says, because a more effective memory-storing mechanism has evolved. "REM sleep could have provided this new mechanism, allowing memory processing to occur 'off-line,'" he suggests. Winson also feels that dreams take visual form because they are evolutionary leftovers, inherited from animals who have no language but rely on vision.

The fact that babies and infants spend more of their time in REM sleep lends support to the theory. According to Winson, this is the time of life when the need to gather, store, and integrate information from the outside world is the greatest. Time spent in REM sleep drops as the organism and its memory system matures.

Freud was at least partly right, Winson says: Dreams do tell people a lot about unconscious mental activity, because they incorporate all the important elements people need for survival—fears, desires, hopes, jealousies, and loves. He believes, however, that Freud was wrong about dreams representing repressed thoughts. In Winson's theory, dreams are difficult to interpret in such a way because they carry such a complex assortment of associations.

In an experiment by Winson that showed a link between theta rhythm and memory, brain surgery that eliminated theta rhythm in rats also weakened the animals' ability to learn spatial information, such as finding a particular location in a maze. During the mid-1970s, Winson identified several regions in the *hippocampus* as sources of theta rhythm. (The hippocampus is a section of the forebrain thought to process short-term memories for long-term storage.)

Winson acknowledges missing parts to his theory. Eliminating theta rhythm during REM sleep in animals has not proved to damage their memory, and the total absence of theta rhythm in primates remains a puzzle. Winson suggests that theta rhythm may have been replaced in higher animals by a different kind of brain activity not yet detected.

As an alternative way of examining dreams, some research does not focus on REM sleep but on the fleeting moments when people slip from waking to stage 1 sleep. At this time, many people experience dreamlike images and sensations, and creative ideas even pop into the mind. The images generated during this half-sleeping period may be the products of a still-active cortex with no sensory input, which thus constructs things from memory until sleep overwhelms it.

While modern dream researchers differ with Freud (and each other) about the function of dreams, most of them do agree with Freud's belief that dreaming opens a window into the unconscious. Future research may tell more about the nature of that window and the reason for dreams.

CHAPTER 7

INSOMNIA AND SLEEP APNEA

Sleep disturbances, and attempts to cure them, are not a new phenomenon. This old advertisement for Dr. Guertin's Nerve Syrup offered a cure for every ailment from epilepsy to insomnia.

At any given time, about 30 million Americans suffer from sleep problems, and these come in a number of forms. The most common problem is *insomnia*—difficulty falling or staying asleep. Many people, however, have the opposite problem: They sleep too much or fall asleep at inappropriate times. The incidence of sleep disorders increases with age, but they can occur at any time of life, even childhood.

Dr. Richard Ferber of the Center for Pediatric Sleep Disorders at Children's Hospital in Boston estimates that more than 25% of children have serious sleep disorders, including nap problems, sleep terrors, sleepwalking, and bedtime difficulties.

Most of these childhood sleep disorders eventually go away, as the child simply grows out of them. Sleep disorders are relatively infrequent in the late teens and early twenties, but their frequency increases again with age.

Insomnia is probably the most common sleep problem. The incidence is higher in older people, but anyone can be sleepless now and then. Insomnia requires special interpretation for children. One problem many parents face (which most children do not regard as a problem) is getting a child to sleep on time. A regular bedtime is essential, and parents can help young children fall asleep by singing, talking, or reading to them. The problem of frequent nighttime awakenings that get parents up should be handled by only brief visits to comfort the child. If parents take a child out of bed to comfort him or her at every awakening, they are actually reinforcing the activity that they are trying to stop.

CAUSES OF INSOMNIA

Everyone has some idea what insomnia is, but medically the condition can be hard to diagnose. Often, the problem is not as severe as the insomniac infers, because he or she interprets disturbed sleep as lack of sleep. A study of hard-core insomniacs at the National Institutes of Health, for example, found that even though patients claimed they barely got a wink of sleep all night, they slept only 43 minutes less on average than a group of normal sleepers. Nevertheless, these people found insomnia to be one of the major problems in their life.

Insomnia can have many causes and take many different forms. Some people cannot sleep at night because of anxiety, others because of involvement in stressful situations. Clinical depression, also called *major affective disorder*, can be an unrecognized cause of insomnia. Overuse of alcohol or drugs can cause insomnia, as can prescription drugs and even substances people do not always realize are drugs— especially the caffeine in coffee, tea, and soft drinks.

"Why doesn't he just snap out of it."

We wouldn't expect someone with a serious physical illness to get better without treatment. Yet, often, for the victims of another disease more widespread than cancer, lung and heart disease combined, treatment is rarely considered.

The disease is mental illness. In fact, of the over 35 million Americans afflicted, only one in five gets treatment. Because their symptoms are either ignored or misread as mere personality problems.

But, mental illness is a medical illness that requires medical attention. Some forms can be caused by a biological disorder. And this new knowledge has led to real progress in the treatment of mental illness. Today, two out of three victims can get better and lead productive lives.

Learn more. For an informative booklet, write: The American Mental Health Fund, P.O. Box 17700, Washington, D.C. 20041. Or call toll free: 1-800-433-5959. In Illinois, call: 1-800-826-2336.

Learn to see the sickness. Learning is the key to healing.

THE AMERICAN MENTAL HEALTH FUND

Insomnia is often caused by mental problems such as stress, depression, or overuse of drugs.

75

In addition, although many adults think alcohol helps them sleep better, an alcoholic stupor is not healthy sleep. Overuse of alcohol shortens sleep and changes its pattern, causing less REM sleep and frequent awakenings during the night. A heavy drinker might get only an hour or two of sleep before waking up and feeling unable to sleep again.

The sleeping pills and tranquilizers many people take can also cause insomnia if overused. For instance, the "rebound effect" occurs when someone who takes a sleep medication for several weeks suffers insomnia when he or she stops using the medication. Some people adjust to the cutoff in a few days, while others suffer insomnia for weeks. For this reason, doctors generally prescribe sleep medications sparingly, for brief periods.

Another problem is *drug dependency insomnia*, which can occur when someone has used a sleeping medication for too long. The drug becomes less effective over time, creating a tendency to increase the dosage. If this continues long enough, sleep can be interrupted by frequent awakenings for another dose of the drug. If the dose then is cut back drastically, the result is persistent awakenings early in the morning.

Probably the most common form of sleeplessness is called *transient psychophysiologic insomnia* (TPI)—*psychophysiologic* means an interaction between the mind and body. Almost every person alive, young or old, has experienced this kind of insomnia, in the form of sleepless hours or a sleepless night on the eve of an important examination or interview or after an argument or other distressing experience. As the word *transient* implies, this sort of insomnia lasts for a relatively brief period. Most people get over their insomnia in a night or two, when the problem causing sleeplessness is solved. If insomnia persists, then treatment may be necessary.

CURES FOR INSOMNIA

If the reason behind a patient's insomnia is clear and the problem is short-term, medication is often the first form of treatment. The physician might prescribe one of the *benzodiazepines*, the family of

This 1889 ad for the Dr. Huber Electro-Magnetic Dry Cell Pocket Medical Battery promised that "electrotherapy" would soothe nerve centers and produce refreshing sleep.

tranquilizers including *Valium* (diazepam) and *Librium* (chlordiaz-epoxide). These drugs have replaced *barbiturates*, which were once the mainstay of insomnia treatment. Although less dangerous than barbiturates, benzodiazepines have side effects of their own and can cause dependence. As noted, the standard recommendation is to take a benzodiazepine or other sleeping pill for the shortest possible time.

Milder drugs that are available without a prescription include some of the *antihistamines* used to treat allergies. Their use in sleep depends on their most notable side effect: drowsiness. The antihistamines are the active ingredients in most over-the-counter sleep medications.

Chronic, or long-term, insomnia is a more difficult problem. Some people suffer insomnia for many months or years. Doctors first look for medical reasons for chronic insomnia, such as hidden psychiatric disorders. Anxiety, depression, and *obsessive-compulsive disorders* (which make sufferers repeat activities such as handwashing over and over again) can cause several different forms of chronic insomnia. Depression causes fragmented sleep, allowing the sufferer to dose off easily but wake up in the early morning hours unable to go back to sleep. Anxiety and obsessive-compulsive disorders make it difficult to fall asleep at all; thoughts race through one's mind and relaxation is impossible.

Winner of the 1986 International Invention Grand Prix, this modern sleeping device, named the Cerebrex, is supposed to overcome both physical and mental fatigue. Its inventor, Dr. Yoshiro Nakamats, claims that one hour inside the device is equal to eight hours of sleep.

Whenever possible, sleep specialists try to avoid the use of drugs to treat chronic insomnia. Their treatment usually starts with an effort to impose good sleep "hygiene" rules. The primary rule is to follow regular hours for going to sleep and waking up. Some people court sleep by staying awake until late at night. Others lie in bed well into the day, tossing sleeplessly for hours. Sleep experts recommend an insomniac go to bed at the same hour every night and stay in bed for a fixed number of hours, seven or eight. This regimen alone helps many sufferers.

Another rule is to use a bed for sleep only. Many people spend a lot of time in bed watching television, eating, or simply worrying. These practices associate bed with waking activities, rather than with sleep. Another sleep hygiene rule is to make the bedroom itself comfortable. A darkened, quiet room at a comfortable temperature is best for sleep, as is a good bed, with a mattress that is not too hard or too soft, too lumpy or too sagging.

Moderate-sized meals at regular intervals are also recommended; for most people, a big meal before bedtime makes sleep more difficult because the digestive system is still hard at work breaking down food. Moderate exercise two to four hours before going to bed is another sleep-inducing method. However, exercise just before bedtime is not advisable because it causes the body to release chemicals that stimulate, rather than relax, the sleeper.

SLEEP APNEA

One form of sleep disorder, *sleep apnea*, causes frequent interruption of breathing during sleep. (*Apnea* means "absence of breathing.") One of its most common symptoms is a specific kind of snoring that occurs tens or hundreds of times during a single night. Each episode lasts 10 to 15 seconds and ends suddenly, often with a physical movement of the whole body.

The snoring is caused by blockage of the breathing passages, and during this time the individual is actually choking; the flow of air to the lungs stops entirely for 10 seconds or more. The episode ends when low levels of oxygen or high levels of carbon dioxide in the blood trigger reflexes that restart breathing. About 1 American in 100 suffers from sleep apnea; as with most sleep disorders, it is more common among older people. One study by Dr. Sonia Ancoli-Israel of the University of California at San Diego found that 24% of 427 people who were 65 and older had some degree of sleep apnea.

In some cases, it appears the frequent stoppage of breathing is serious enough to cause physical or mental problems, although the relationship between sleep apnea and such problems is not clear. For example, some studies have discovered an increased incidence of deaths from heart attacks in sleep apnea patients. In a 1990 study of 223 patients, Dr. Bernard Burack of Montefiore Medical Center in New York found evidence that sleep apnea doubled the risk of death from heart disease. In addition, other studies found sleep apnea patients more likely to have auto crashes and other accidents because the condition reduces alertness, although some studies have not shown such relationships.

Dr. Donald L. Bliwise of Stanford Medical School suggests a link between sleep apnea and mental impairment in elderly people. His

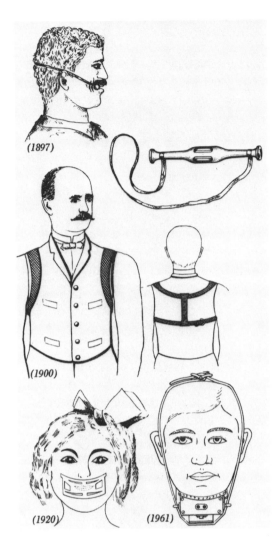

The sleep disturbance known as sleep apnea is marked by excessive snoring caused by short bouts of choking. Over the years, a variety of devices have been designed to help sleepers overcome both snoring and sleep apnea.

(1897)

(1900)

(1920)

(1961)

five-year study showed a steady decline in performance on several mental tests in sleep apnea patients.

The repeated awakenings that occur in sleep apnea clearly disrupt the normal pattern of sleep and diminish both the amount of deep sleep and REM sleep. Thus, people with sleep apnea find themselves feeling listless, sleepy, and irritable during the day.

Sleep apnea usually is brought on by a physical problem. In children, sleep apnea can be caused by enlarged tonsils or adenoids or repeated infections of the throat or middle ear, all of which block the airway. In middle age, sleep apnea occurs when muscles of the soft palate at the base of the tongue and the *uvula* (the conical, fleshy structure hanging from the center of the soft palate) relax and sag repeatedly. The disorder is especially common in overweight people, because excess fat narrows the breathing passage.

"A weight loss of 10% to 15% invariably improves sleep apnea" in these patients, says Dr. Philip Smith, director of the sleep disorders center at Johns Hopkins University. "A 300-pound person who loses 30 pounds gets the same benefit as a 200-pound person who loses 20 pounds."

Another general recommendation is that patients limit use of sedatives and alcohol, and for some individuals a change in sleeping posture

Unlike insomnia, which may be caused by mental stress, sleep apnea is caused by a physical obstruction in the airway. The problem can occur, for example, when muscles in the soft palate at the base of the tongue and the uvula relax and sag, blocking breathing passages during sleep.

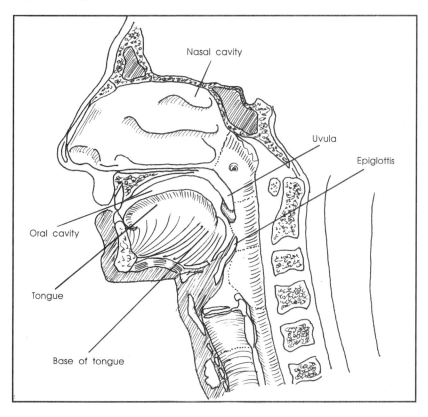

is advised, because sleep apnea is more common in people who sleep on their backs. One old-fashioned informal treatment for snoring is to tape a tennis ball to the snorer's back, making the supine position too uncomfortable to maintain.

A more modern technique was used in a 1989 study by Dr. Rosalind Cartwright at Rush-Presbyterian-St. Luke's Hospital in Chicago. In this study, 60 sleep apnea patients were outfitted with chest beepers that went off 15 seconds after they began snoring while lying on their backs. The patients were trained to roll over to their sides when the beeper went off, which reduced sleep apnea episodes from an average of more than 50 an hour to fewer than 5 an hour.

Currently the most effective therapy for severe sleep apnea is *continuous positive airway pressure* (CPAP). A mask worn over the face connects to a compressor that forces air through the nasal passages into the airway. Other options include a retaining device that prevents the tongue from blocking the airway; a jaw device that keeps the airway open; tubes that bring air in through the nose (but are uncomfortable to wear); and a cervical collar to prevent bending of the neck, which can also block the airway.

Surgery can also help. In children with sleep apnea, once enlarged adenoids or tonsils are removed, the problem is cured. Adults with severe sleep apnea can undergo surgery to reduce tissue that blocks the airway, but that treatment is reserved for patients who cannot be helped by other methods.

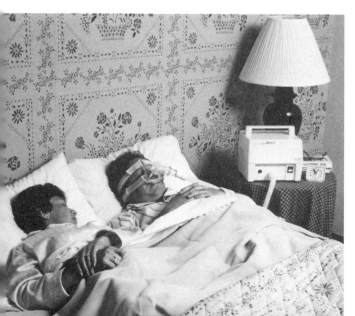

One of the most effective nonsurgical treatments for sleep apnea involves wearing a mask that forces the sleeper to breathe through the nose. However, in more serious cases, surgery may be necessary.

CHAPTER 8

NARCOLEPSY AND OTHER SLEEP DISORDERS

This depiction of overwhelming sleep actually represents a serious problem. One out of every 1,000 people suffers from the sleep disorder known as narcolepsy.

One of the most common sleep disorders is *narcolepsy*, a condition in which people either feel drowsy all the time or fall asleep suddenly for a few minutes at a time. It occurs in about 1 out of every 1,000 people, affecting men and women equally. Narcolepsy usually starts in the teens or twenties and worsens with age.

A narcoleptic who falls asleep may fall over due to *cataplexy*, a loss of muscle tone that prevents the individual from maintaining an upright position. About 80% of narcoleptics also suffer from this problem. A smaller number of patients experience two other symptoms: menacing or frightening hallucinations that occur at the onset of a sleep attack and an odd sort of sleep paralysis in which the mind remains awake, but the body refuses to move. Such an episode can last from 1 or 2 minutes up to 10 minutes. Touching or shaking the patient can end the paralysis. Some patients also have periods during which they perform complex automatic acts—writing, speaking, or even driving in a mechanical fashion—but retain no memory of these actions. All of these symptoms—sleep attacks, hallucinations, and sleep paralysis—can occur in rapid succession.

NARCOLEPSY RESEARCH

The brain waves observed during narcoleptic sleep attacks are similar to those seen during REM sleep. This suggests that narcolepsy is caused by an abnormality of the brain mechanisms controlling REM sleep. Most likely, the centers that ordinarily suppress REM sleep stop functioning normally. The fact that narcoleptics go straight into REM sleep at night, rather than following the normal cycle of sleep stages, supports this belief. Narcoleptic sleep attacks also occur at 90- to 100-minute intervals during the day, the same cycles as REM sleep periods at night. In addition, sleep attacks are often precipitated by strong emotions, such as anger.

Studies indicate that narcolepsy has some genetic component. Almost half of the patients suffering from the disorder have a close relative who is also affected by the condition. A Japanese researcher, Dr. Yutaka Honda, found that almost all narcoleptics have the same gene, called HLA-DR2, which regulates part of the immune response. Although this does not mean that the gene causes narcolepsy, it suggests that HLA-DR2 could be close to another gene that is involved in the cause. However, it appears that narcolepsy is not always inherited. Some people with the disorder do not carry the HLA-DR2 gene, and some evidence shows it can follow head injuries or diseases that cause brain damage.

Merrill M. Mitler of the Sleep Disorders Center at the Scripps Clinic in La Jolla, California, believes narcolepsy could be an *autoimmune disease*, a condition in which the body's immune system mistakenly attacks its own tissue. The HLA-DR2 work points in that direction, he says, but the theory needs more proof.

Much narcolepsy research is being performed on dogs, who can suffer essentially the same disease as humans. Canine narcoleptics have the same brain-wave pattern as humans and are helped by the same drugs used to treat people. In a few breeds, such as Labrador retrievers and Doberman pinschers, narcolepsy is passed from generation to generation in a pattern indicating that it comes from a single gene. Research on the brain stems of these dogs shows an excess number of receptors for acetylcholine, the neurotransmitter that turns off REM sleep, though it is not known how this is connected to narcolepsy. In addition, these animals have a shortage of *dopamine* and norepinephrine, the neurotransmitters that also repress REM sleep.

Narcolepsy is usually treated with drugs that act on these neurotransmitter systems. Doctors prescribe two kinds of medications—stimulants that reduce the tendency to fall asleep and compounds known to suppress REM sleep. *Methylphenidate* is one type of stimulant often prescribed. Amphetamines are another standby. Both of these types of drugs are prescribed specifically to prevent sleep attacks. They probably act by increasing the availability of dopamine, the neurotransmitter used by one of the brain stem centers to inhibit REM sleep.

Antidepressant drugs are prescribed for cataplexy. Although they have no effect on sleep attacks, they are believed to increase the availability of norepinephrine, the REM-repressing neurotransmitter. In addition to drug treatment, patients can also be helped by taking brief naps on a carefully planned schedule during the day.

HYPERSOMNIA

Another form of excess sleepiness goes by the name of *hypersomnia*, which simply means "too much sleep." The most common form is *idiopathic hypersomnia*, which means "excess sleepiness of unknown cause."

Patients with hypersomnia complain they feel sleepy throughout the day. They are often compelled to take naps, which can last for several hours but are not refreshing, and nighttime sleep is sometimes prolonged. Sometimes they can sleep for several days, almost without interruption. People with this condition experience more deep sleep, rather than REM sleep, and often remain confused and drowsy even

Many people suffer from drowsiness during daytime hours, but often the problem is not a medical one. Although many individuals believe the ideal amount of sleep averages eight hours every night, very few actually get that. Most people feel they do not have enough waking hours to get everything done, making sleep a low priority.

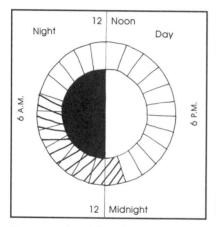

Sleep cycle of the student

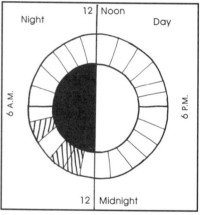

Sleep cycle of the doctor

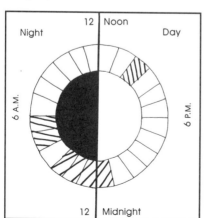

Sleep cycle of the mother

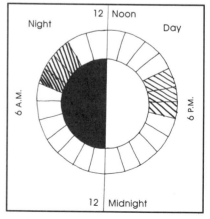

Sleep cycle of the trucker

when not asleep. Physical activity reduces tiredness, but heavy meals and monotonous activities increase it.

Like narcolepsy, hypersomnia usually develops during the teen years. Also like narcolepsy, hypersomnia seems to run in families, and the incidence of either one of these conditions is higher in families where the other also occurs. As with narcolepsy, hypersomnia is believed to be a disorder of the neurotransmitter system. Studies have shown that hypersomnia patients use up dopamine at an especially high rate. Despite the similarities between hypersomnia and narcolepsy, however, they remain distinctly different. For example, the high incidence of the HLA-DR2 gene seen in narcolepsy does not appear at all in hypersomnia.

Another form of the condition is *periodic hypersomnia*. Patients suffering from this disorder usually go for weeks or months with normal sleeping patterns, then experience periods of excessive sleep that may last from one day up to several weeks. In women, periodic hypersomnia can be related to the menstrual cycle, though the brain mechanisms behind the condition are not known. Doctors treat it with the same stimulant drugs used for narcolepsy, but with limited success.

DAYTIME SLEEPINESS

Cases of daytime sleepiness can be related to a number of conditions, some of which have already been discussed. Although depression can cause insomnia, some forms of depression cause hypersomnia, which is often prolonged well into the day. Excess sleepiness can also be due to less serious psychological problems. Staying asleep is one good way to escape everyday problems. While some people react to stress by staying awake, others pull the covers over their heads and remain in bed. This type of hypersomnia usually disappears when the problem is resolved or goes away.

People who suffer from sleep apnea are likely to feel sleepy during the day because they get less good-quality sleep at night. The same is true of persons who suffer from nocturnal myoclonus, the condition that causes frequent, involuntary movements of the legs during the night. These kicks and twitches can wake sleepers every few minutes, so they rise from bed weary and unrefreshed.

Another nighttime condition that leads to daytime sleepiness goes by the name of *gastroesophageal reflex*, commonly known as heartburn. The burning feeling is caused by acidic digestive juices that the stomach washes into the throat when the valve that is supposed to hold them back closes inadequately. Heartburn is more likely to occur when a person lies down, because acid flows more readily when the body is in a horizontal position. Antacids that control heartburn can make sleep more refreshing.

Sleeping pills that help a person sleep at night can also cause drowsiness during the daytime, because the drug can remain active for a number of hours. Drug-related daytime sleepiness is particularly common among older people, partly because their bodies do not metabolize these medications efficiently. Additionally, older people are more likely to take drugs that may interfere with sleep, such as antidepressants, painkillers, antihistamines, and drugs for high blood pressure. Some older people may take several of these medications simultaneously for various medical conditions.

As mentioned earlier, alcohol can also interfere with sleep. Individuals who drink too much tend to fall asleep, day or night. Because

Another cause of daytime drowsiness is linked to sleeping pills. They may help a sleepless person at night but can continue to cause drowsiness the next day. Another misconception about sleep aids concerns the use of alcohol, which contrary to popular opinion often makes sleep less restful.

a drunken stupor is not a refreshing kind of sleep, it can be disabling during the day. Older people may be more vulnerable to relatively small amounts of alcohol because they may be taking medications, such as tranquilizers, that increase sleepiness when combined with alcohol.

Another cause of daytime sleepiness is nighttime shift work. A 1989 study by Mark Rosekind, a psychologist at Stanford University, found that many night workers never adjust to their schedule. On their nights off, the workers Rosekind observed followed a day worker's schedule, staying up during the day and sleeping at night. As a result, they were sleepy much of the time. Older people appear particularly prone to this problem, since their circadian rhythms typically do not adjust as well to shift work as those of younger people.

Kleine-Levin Syndrome

A rare condition called *Kleine-Levin syndrome* combines periodic hypersomnia with periods of binge eating. Two or three of these attacks occur during the year, each lasting a week or two. Kleine-Levin syndrome first appears in young males aged 10 to 21, but the symptoms lessen over the years and usually disappear by middle age.

PARASOMNIAS

A grab-bag of sleep disorders—including jet lag, bed-wetting, sleep-walking, myoclonus, night terrors, and tooth-grinding—fall under the name of *parasomnias*. Sleep-related headaches are also classified as parasomnias.

Headaches

Migraine headaches (intense headaches that recur periodically and typically occur on only one side of the head) usually begin during sleep. The same is true of *cluster headaches*, which are especially painful and get their name because they recur periodically for hours after an attack begins. Cluster headaches begin during or immediately after REM sleep. The patient (most often a male) wakes up with nausea, severe pain, a runny nose, and tears running from the eyes. The attack lasts from 30 minutes to several hours. Later attacks also occur during REM sleep periods. A similar kind of headache, *paroxysmal hemicrania* (headaches that occur only in one side of the head) have more frequent but briefer attacks that last 15 minutes and also are associated with REM sleep.

Sleep Phase Disorders

Another set of problems occurs when the body's internal clock is out of sync with the 24-hour day. Jet lag and sleep problems caused by shift work have already been mentioned in Chapter 2. Still other sleep phase disorders have a natural cause. Without outside cues given by the day-night cycle, most people sleep on a 25-hour schedule. In *hyper-nyctohemeral syndrome*, the body does not respond to these cues as it should. The patient sleeps and wakes by a 25- to 27-hour schedule. Efforts to train these patients to live by the normal 24-hour schedule usually have only limited success.

A person suffering from *delayed sleep-phase syndrome* falls asleep a little later every night—11:00 P.M. one night, 11:20 P.M. the next night, 11:40 P.M. the third night, and so on. Eventually, he or she may have difficulty falling asleep until the early morning hours and as a result have trouble getting up on time. Victims of *advanced sleep-phase syndrome* go to sleep a little earlier every night. Most of the time, these disorders occur in a mild form that leaves people just a bit uncomfortable with the normal sleep schedule.

REM sleep behavior disorder (see Chapter 1) is another phase problem. Research indicates that treatment with a benzodiazepine tranquilizer may help.

In recent years, researchers have become aware of sleep problems caused by *posttraumatic stress disorder*, a long-term reaction to a horrible experience such as a kidnapping, internment in a concentration camp, or wartime combat. Affected people relive their dreadful experiences during sleep, sometimes acting them out. These are not dreams, since they occur during non-REM sleep. Patients can be helped by psychiatric counseling and by taking benzodiazepines.

VISITING A SLEEP CENTER

Over the past two decades, a new medical discipline was created to deal with insomnia and other sleep problems. While most family physicians can deal with temporary bouts of insomnia, a visit to a physician or center that specializes in sleep disorders may sometimes be necessary when insomnia becomes chronic.

A visit to a sleep disorders center generally begins with the physician taking a sleep history. The doctor asks questions about existing sleep patterns, drug use, and possible medical and emotional problems underlying sleep disorders. Patients may be asked to take one or more standard psychological tests. After recording an individual's medical history, the next step is often an all-night sleep study.

For the study, the patient goes to the center an hour or two before normal bedtime to be hooked up to a *polysomnograph*, a device that records physical and neurological events during sleep. Experts attach electrodes to the head, the side of the face, the chest, and the legs to record brain waves, eye movements, and muscle activity. Breathing

This electroencephalograph at the Georgetown University Sleep Center is equipped with a monitor to record every aspect of an individual's movement during sleep. Such machinery is generally positioned in a centralized control area, separate from the rooms where patients sleep.

In addition to traditional treatments for sleep problems, such as medication, many sleep centers use biofeedback to help patients learn to relax. This technique applies the theory that a person can improve his or her physical condition through mental concentration.

and pulse rate during sleep are also measured, and blood oxygen content may also be measured by a clip attached to a finger or ear. Readings are collected throughout the night.

After gathering all the data from personal history, psychological tests, and the polysomnograph, the physician will make a diagnosis and prescribe a course of action to relieve the problem. The treatment may include sleep hygiene measures, some use of medications, and even relaxation training and *biofeedback*. (Biofeedback is a technique using the senses to consciously control involuntary bodily processes.)

The American Sleep Disorders Association sets standards for the more than 700 sleep centers in the United States. To be fully accredited by the society, a center must have a physician who specializes in sleep medicine and a trained technician to operate the polysomnograph. Accredited sleep centers must also offer each patient a private bedroom, at least 8 by 10 feet in size, with a centralized control room for monitoring equipment.

In addition, an approved center must keep full records of all patients and be affiliated with a medical facility offering general care, such as a university-based hospital. Only about a quarter of the centers with sleep diagnostic services meet all those standards. However, some centers qualify for partial accreditation.

As scientists learn about the processes of sleep, more can be done to ensure that people will get the rest that is essential for a healthy mind and body.

APPENDIX:
FOR MORE INFORMATION

The following is a list of organizations and associations in the United States and Canada that can provide further information about sleep disorders and related topics.

GENERAL INFORMATION

CANADA

Sleep/Wake Disorders Canada
Box 223, Station S
Toronto, Ontario
M5M 4L7
Canada
(416) 398-1627

Sunnybrook Health Science Center
University of Toronto
2075 Bayview Avenue
Toronto, Ontario
M4N 3M5
Canada
(416) 480-4693

UNITED STATES

The following sleep disorders clinics are accredited by the American Sleep Disorders Association.

American Sleep Disorders Association
604 Second Street SW
Rochester, MN 55902
(507) 287-6006

ALABAMA

Sleep Disorders Center of Alabama
800 Montclair Road
Birmingham, AL 35213
(205) 592-5650

ARIZONA

Sleep Disorders Center
Good Samaritan Medical Center
1111 East McDowell Road
Phoenix, AZ 85006
(602) 239-5815

ARKANSAS

Sleep Disorders Center
Baptist Medical Center
9601 I-630
Little Rock, AR 72205-7299
(501) 227-1902

CALIFORNIA

Stanford Sleep Disorders Clinic
211 Quarry Road
Hoover Pavilion, Room N2A
Stanford, CA 94305-5573

(415) 723-6601
(415) 723-6095

UCLA Sleep Disorders Center
Department of Neurology
710 Westwood Plaza, Room 1155
Los Angeles, CA 90024
(213) 206-8005

COLORADO

Sleep Disorders Center
Presbyterian Medical Center
1719 East 19th Avenue
Denver, CO 80218
(303) 839-6447

CONNECTICUT

New Haven Sleep Disorders Center
100 York Street, Suite 2G
New Haven, CT 06511
(203) 776-9578

FLORIDA

Sleep Disorders Center
Mt. Sinai Medical Center
4300 Alton Road
Miami Beach, FL 33140
(305) 674-2613

GEORGIA

Sleep Disorders Center
Northside Hospital
1000 Johnson Ferry Road
Atlanta, GA 30342
(404) 256-8977

ILLINOIS

Sleep Disorders Center
Methodist Medical Center of Illinois
221 NE Glen Oak
Peoria, IL 61636

(309) 672-4966
(diagnosis and treatment only)

Sleep Disorders Center
Rush-Presbyterian-Saint Luke's
1753 West Congress Parkway
Chicago, IL 60612
(312) 942-5440

Sleep Disorders Center
University of Chicago
5841 South Maryland Avenue
Box 237
Chicago, IL 60637
(312) 702-0648

INDIANA

Sleep Disorders Center
Winona Memorial Hospital
3232 North Meridian Street
Indianapolis, IN 46208
(317) 927-2100

KENTUCKY

Sleep Disorders Center
Humana Hospital Audubon
One Audubon Plaza Drive
Louisville, KY 40217
(502) 636-7459

LOUISIANA

Department of Psychiatry and
   Neurology
1415 Tulane Avenue
New Orleans, LA 70112
(504) 584-3592

MARYLAND

Johns Hopkins Sleep Disorders Center
Francis Scott Key Medical Center
Asthma and Allergy Building, 4th floor
301 Bayview Blvd.

Baltimore, MD 21224
(301) 550-0571

National Capital Sleep Center
4520 East-West Highway, Suite 510
Bethesda, MD 21224
(301) 656-9515

MICHIGAN

Sleep Disorders and Research Center
Henry Ford Hospital
2921 West Grand Blvd.
Detroit, MI 48202
(313) 972-1800

MINNESOTA

Sleep Disorders Center
Hennepin County Medical Center
Minneapolis, MN 55415
(612) 347-6288

Sleep Disorders Center
Mayo Clinic
200 First Street SW
Rochester, MN 55905
(507) 385-4150

Sleep Disorders Center
Methodist Hospital
6500 Excelsior Blvd.
Minneapolis, MN 55426
(612) 932-6083

MISSISSIPPI

Sleep Disorders Center
Division of Somnology
University of Mississippi
Jackson, MS 39216
(601) 984-4820

MISSOURI

Sleep Disorders Center
Deaconess Hospital

6150 Oakland Avenue
St. Louis, MO 63139
(314) 768-3100

NEBRASKA

Sleep Disorders Center
Lutheran Medical Center
515 South 26th Street
Omaha, NE 68103
(402) 536-6352

NEW HAMPSHIRE

Sleep Disorders Center
Dartmouth Hitchcock Medical Center
703 Remsen Building
Hanover, NH 03756
(603) 646-7534

NEW YORK

Sleep Disorders Center
Columbia-Presbyterian Medical Center
161 Fort Washington Avenue
New York, NY 10032
(212) 305-1860
(treatment only)

Sleep Disorders Center
Department of Psychiatry
SUNY at Stony Brook
Stony Brook, NY 11794
(516) 444-2916
(diagnosis only)

Sleep-Wake Disorders Center
Montefiore Hospital
111 East 210th Street
Bronx, NY 10467
(212) 920-4841

NORTH CAROLINA

Sleep Disorders Center
University Memorial Hospital

P.O. Box 560727
Charlotte, NC 28256
(704) 548-5855

NORTH DAKOTA

TNI Sleep Disorders Center
720 4th Street North
Fargo, ND 58122
(701) 234-5673

OHIO

Sleep Disorders Center
Department of Neurology
Cleveland Clinic
Cleveland, OH 44106
(216) 444-8732

Sleep Disorders Evaluation Center
Department of Psychiatry
Ohio State University
Columbus, OH 43210
(614) 293-8296

OKLAHOMA

Sleep Disorders Center
Presbyterian Hospital
700 NE 13th Street
Oklahoma City, OK 73104
(405) 271-6312

OREGON

Pacific Northwest Sleep/Wake
    Disorders Program
1130 NW 22nd Avenue, Suite 240
Portland, OR 97210
(503) 229-8311

PENNSYLVANIA

Sleep Disorders Center
Department of Neurology

Crozer-Chester Medical Center
Upland-Chester, PA 19013
(215) 447-2689

Sleep Disorders Center
The Medical College of Pennsylvania
3300 Henry Avenue
Philadelphia, PA 19129
(215) 842-4250

Sleep Disorders Center
Western Psychiatric Institute
3811 O'Hara Street
Pittsburgh, PA 15213
(412) 624-2246
(diagnosis, treatment, and
    research only)

SOUTH CAROLINA

Sleep Disorders Center
Baptist Medical Center
Taylor at Marion Streets
Columbia, SC 29220
(803) 771-5847

TENNESSEE

BMH Sleep Disorders Center
Baptist Memorial Hospital
899 Madison Avenue
Memphis, TN 38146
(901) 522-5704

TEXAS

Sleep Disorders Center
All Saints Episcopal Hospital
1400 Eighth Avenue
Fort Worth, TX 76101
(817) 927-6120

Sleep Disorders Center
Department of Psychiatry
Baylor College of Medicine

Houston, TX 77030
(713) 798-4886

Sleep-Wake Disorders Center
Presbyterian Hospital
8200 Walnut Hill Lane
Dallas, TX 75213
(214) 696-8563

UTAH

Intermountain Sleep Disorders Center
LDS Hospital
325 Eighth Avenue
Salt Lake City, UT 84143
(801) 321-3617

VIRGINIA

Sleep Disorders Center
Norfolk General Hospital
600 Gresham Drive
Norfolk, VA 23507
(804) 628-3322

WISCONSIN

Sleep Disorders Center
Columbia Hospital
2025 East Newport Avenue
Milwaukee, WI 53211
(414) 961-4650

DREAMS

Association for the Study of Dreams
P.O. Box 1600
Vienna, VA 22183
(703) 242-8888

NARCOLEPSY

American Narcolepsy Association
P.O. Box 1187
San Carlos, CA 94070
(415) 591-7979

Narcolepsy and Cataplexy Foundation
of America (NCFA)
1410 York Avenue, Suite 4D
New York, NY 10021
(212) 628-6315

SUDDEN INFANT DEATH SYNDROME

Canadian Foundation for the Study of
Infant Deaths
SIDS Foundation
P.O. Box 190, Station R
Toronto, Ontario
M4G 3Z9
Canada
(416) 488-3260

National Sudden Infant Death
Syndrome Clearinghouse
(NSIDSC)
8201 Greensboro Drive, Suite 600
McLean, VA 22102
(703) 821-8955

SIDS Alliance
10500 Little Patuxent Parkway
Suite 420
Columbia, MD 21044
(301) 964-8000

FURTHER READING

GENERAL INFORMATION

The American Medical Association Straight Talk No-Nonsense Guide to Better Sleep. New York: Random House, 1984.

Arkin, Arthur M. *Sleep-Talking: Psychology and Psychophysiology.* Hillsdale, NJ: Earlbaum, Lawrence, 1982.

Borberly, Alexander. *Secrets of Sleep.* New York: Basic Books, 1986.

Czeisler, Charles A., and Christian Guilleminault, eds. *REM Sleep: Its Temporal Distribution.* New York: Raven Press, 1980.

Dement, William C. *Some Must Watch While Some Must Sleep: Exploring the World of Sleep.* New York: Norton, 1978.

Drucker-Colin, Rene, et al., eds. *The Functions of Sleep.* San Diego, CA: Academic Press, 1979.

Ford, Norman. *Good Night: The Easy and Natural Way to Sleep the Whole Night Through.* Gloucester, MA: Para Research, 1983.

———. *Sleep Well, Live Well.* New York: Zebra Books, 1985.

Guilleminault, Christian, ed. *Sleep and Its Disorders in Children.* New York: Raven Press, 1987.

————. *Sleeping and Waking Disorders: Indications and Techniques.* Stoneham, MA: Butterworth, 1982.

Hales, Dianne. *How to Sleep like a Baby, Wake Up Refreshed, and Get More out of Life.* New York: Ballantine Books, 1987.

Horne, James. *Why We Sleep: The Functions of Sleep in Human and Other Mammals.* New York: Oxford University Press, 1988.

Karacan, Ismet, ed. *Psychophysiological Aspects of Sleep.* Park Ridge, NJ: Noyes Publications, 1981.

Kleitman, Nathaniel. *Sleep and Wakefulness.* Chicago: University of Chicago Press, 1987.

Lamberg, Lynne. *Drugs and Sleep.* New York: Chelsea House, 1988.

————. *Guide to Better Sleep.* New York: Random House, 1984.

Mendelson, Wallace B., et al., eds. *Human Sleep and Its Disorders.* New York: Plenum, 1977.

Parkes, J. D. *Sleep and Its Disorders.* Philadelphia: Saunders, 1986.

Research and Education Association Staff. *Sleep and Dream Research.* Piscataway, NJ: Research and Education Association, 1982.

Sartre, Jean-Paul. *Troubled Sleep.* New York: Random House, 1972.

Wauquier, A., et al., eds. *Sleep: Neurotransmitters and Neuromodulators.* New York: Raven Press, 1985.

DREAMS

Freud, Sigmund. *The Interpretation of Dreams.* Translated by James Strachey. New York: Avon Books, 1965.

Gackenbach, Jayne, ed. *Sleep and Dreams: A Sourcebook.* New York: Garland, 1985.

Gutheil, Emil. *Handbook of Dream Analysis.* New York: Liveright, 1970.

Hobson, J. Allan. *The Dreaming Brain.* New York: Basic Books, 1988.

Jones, Richard M. *The New Psychology of Dreaming.* Orlando: Grune & Stratton, 1970.

Kramer, Milton. *Dream Psychology and the New Biology of Dreaming.* Springfield, IL: Thomas, 1969.

LaBerge, Stephen. *Lucid Dreaming.* New York: Ballantine Books, 1985.

Miller, Gustavus H. *The Dictionary of Dreams: Ten Thousand Dreams Interpreted.* New York: Arco, 1987.

Quinn, Adrienne. *Dreams of History That Came True.* Tacoma, WA: Dream Research, 1987.

Silverstein, Alvin, and Virginia Silverstein. *Sleep and Dreams.* New York: HarperCollins, 1974.

Tanner, Wilda B. *The Mystical, Magical, Marvelous World of Dreams.* Tahlequah, OK: Sparrow Hawk Press, 1988.

HIBERNATION

Lyman, Charles, et al. *Hibernation and Torpor in Mammals and Birds.* New York: Academic Press, 1982.

INSOMNIA

Coleman, Richard. *Wide Awake at Three A.M. by Choice or by Chance.* San Francisco: Freeman, 1986.

Dooley, Tricia C. *Insomnia: Index of Modern Information*. Annandale: ABBE Publishing Association of Washington, DC, 1988.

Dryer, Bernard, and Ellen S. Kaplan. *Inside Insomnia: How to Get a Good Night's Sleep*. New York: Random House, 1986.

Flatto, Janice S. *Why Some People Can't Sleep*. Miami: Plymouth Press, 1985.

Hartmann, Ernest. *The Sleeping Pill*. New Haven: Yale University Press, 1978.

Kales, Anthony, and Joyce D. Kales. *Evaluation and Treatment of Insomnia*. New York: Oxford University Press, 1984.

Sweeney, Donald R. *Overcoming Insomnia: A Medical Program for Problem Sleepers*. New York: Putnam, 1989.

SNORING

Boulware, Marcus. *Snoring*. Rockaway, NJ: American Faculty Press, 1974.

Fairbanks, David N., et al. *Snoring and Obstructive Sleep Apnea*. New York: Raven Press, 1987.

Fletcher, Eugene C., ed. *Abnormalities of Respiration During Sleep: Diagnosis, Pathophysiology*. Orlando: Grune & Stratton, 1986.

Rosenthal, Lois. *How to Stop Snoring*. Cincinnati: Writers Digest Books, 1986.

GLOSSARY

acetylcholine a neurotransmitter used by the nerve cells of the pons that control the REM stage of sleep

antihistamines compounds used to treat allergic reactions, cold symptoms, and motion sickness; tend to cause drowsiness

barbiturates drugs causing depression of the central nervous system; generally used to reduce anxiety or to induce euphoria

benzodiazepines a family of tranquilizers—including Valium and Librium—that relieve anxiety, relax muscles, and have sedative and hypnotic effects

brain stem a three-inch span of nerve fibers that connects the brain to the spinal cord

brain waves electrical activity in the brain; detectable by electrodes

bruxism the habit of unconsciously grinding or gritting the teeth, especially during sleep or in stressful situations

cataplexy an aftermath of fright, shock, or anger that results in sudden loss of muscle functions despite retention of full consciousness

cerebral hemisphere either of two halves of the cerebrum; the left hemisphere is associated with orderly thinking; the right hemisphere is associated with nonverbal responses

cerebrum the top portion of the brain; responsible for conscious mental processes

chronobiologists scientists who study the effect of time on living systems

circadian rhythms rhythms occurring in an organism on a 24-hour cycle

cytokines infection-fighting compounds produced by the body's immune system; certain compounds, such as muramyl dipeptide, act through certain cytokines to create sleepiness

dormancy a state of suspended activity common to some some animals; differs from sleep in that the brain-wave patterns typical of sleep are not detected in a dormant animal

DSIP delta sleep-inducing peptide; a peptide (or small protein) that once injected causes animals to fall quickly into deep non-REM sleep

EEG electroencephalogram; a recording of electrical activity in the brain; electrodes attached to the head produce graphs of brain-wave activity on a computer screen or printout

enuresis involuntary urination; bedwetting

EOG electrooculograph; an instrument used to detect the electrical signals generated by eye movements

epidemiologists scientists who study the incidence, distribution, and control of disease in a population

forebrain the upper section of the brain containing the cerebrum

hibernation deep torpor; the passing of winter by certain animals in a resting state in which body temperature and metabolic rate drop to nearly zero and the brain shows no sign of activity

hypernyctohemeral syndrome a condition that causes individuals to sleep and wake on a 25- or 27-hour schedule

hypersomnia a sleep disorder in which sufferers sleep too much and experience more deep sleep than REM sleep

hypothalamus the portion of the cerebrum that regulates body temperature, breathing rate, hunger, and thirst and influences blood pressure and the development of secondary sex characteristics

insomnia an inability to sleep or stay asleep; the most frequent causes of insomnia are anxiety and pain

interleukin-1 a chemical, made by the body, involved in the regulation of the immune system; a cytokine that induces sleep

Kleine-Levin syndrome periods of excessive sleep and overeating that may last for several weeks and that usually occur in adolescent boys

L-tryptophan a substance found in lecithin thought to reduce insomnia

luteinizing hormone a hormone from the pituitary gland that stimulates the sexual organs to mature

MDP muramyl dipeptide; a sleep substance that causes larger-than-usual amounts of non-REM sleep when injected into animals; MDP also raises body temperature and activates the immune system

medulla the part of the brain containing centers that control involuntary functions

metabolic rate the rate at which the body uses energy

midbrain the part of the brain containing centers that receive messages from the inner ear, the eyes, and the cerebrum; helps control sleep

muramyl peptide Factor S; a substance produced by the destruction and digestion of bacteria by white blood cells; found in the cerebrospinal fluid of goats and in human urine; when injected with a small dose of the substance, animal test subjects, such as rabbits, will sleep for as long as six hours in non-REM sleep

myoclonus irregular, involuntary twitching or contraction of a muscle or group of muscles

narcolepsy a condition characterized by recurrent, uncontrollable brief attacks of sleep

neural garbage collection a theory suggesting that dreams are the brain's way of getting rid of unwanted information

neurons cells that carry electrical messages throughout the body

neurotransmitter a chemical that carries nerve signals across gaps between nerve cells or between nerve cells and muscle cells; serotonin and norepinephrine are two neurotransmitters that play major roles in the body's sleep centers; acetylcholine is a neurotransmitter that promotes REM sleep

night terrors the sudden awakening of a child in dazed terror

nocturnal myoclonus the twitching or contracting of a muscle or group of muscles during the night

norepinephrine a neurotransmitter located in the brain that has been found to be connected with muscle tone during REM sleep

pharynx the membranous passage located at the back of the throat that connects the esophagus and the trachea (windpipe); during sleep, the muscles that line the pharynx relax, causing some people to snore

phisostigmine a drug that mimics acetylcholine; can induce REM sleep

pituitary gland a small gland in the brain that controls various hormones that regulate body functions and growth

pons the part of the brain stem with centers that control REM and non-REM sleep; also responsible for the rapid eye movement of REM sleep

prolactin a hormone that stimulates milk production in females

prostaglandin D$_2$ a group of fatty acid derivatives that controls blood pressure and smooth muscle contraction; a cytokine that enhances sleep

putative sleep subtance commonly accepted sleep inducers such as sleeping pills

REM sleep a stage of sleep during which brain waves are slow and the sleeper experiences rapid eye movement and irregular heart rate and respiration; the only stage of sleep in which dreams occur

REM sleep behavior disorder a sleep ailment, usually occurring in males over 50, that causes them to perform during sleep the activities they are dreaming about

sensory perception the acknowledgment of stimuli by the five senses

serotonin a neurotransmitter found in the brain that is acquired through the consumption of certain foods; affects the brain's level of alertness

shallow torpor a state of mental and motor inactivity with little breathing, occurring in some small mammals and birds

SIDS sudden infant death syndrome; crib death; the unexplained death of an apparently healthy baby, usually occuring between the second week and first year of life

sleep apnea the periodic cessation of breathing during sleep; characterized by episodes of snoring that end suddenly; often accompanied by physical movement of the whole body

SPS sleep-promoting substance; a mixture of four compounds taken from rats that makes animals sleep longer by increasing the amount of REM sleep

suprachiasmatic nucleus the region in the hypothalamus that controls the sleep-waking cycle

thalamus the part of the forebrain that processes incoming stimuli and then sends appropriate signals to other sections of the brain

theta rhythm a high amplitude brain wave of six cycles per second produced by the brains of lower mammals and rodents during waking hours and REM sleep

theta waves the brain waves detected on an EEG that define stage 1 sleep

thyroid a gland that helps regulate the body's use of energy

thyrotropin a thyroid-stimulating hormone; secreted by the pituitary gland that regulates the secretion of thyroid hormones

type II interferon a disease-fighting protein; a cytokine that induces sleep

zeitgebers external signals that set the body's biological clock

INDEX

PICTURE CREDITS

Edward Edelson is former science editor of the *New York Daily News* and past president of the National Association of Science Writers. His books include *The ABC's of Prescription Narcotics* and the textbook *Chemical Principles*. He has won awards for his writing from such groups as the American Heart Association, the American Cancer Society, the American Academy of Pediatrics, and the American Psychological Society.

Dale C. Garell, M.D., is medical director of California Children Services, Department of Health Services, County of Los Angeles. He is also associate dean for curriculum at the University of Southern California School of Medicine and clinical professor in the Department of Pediatrics & Family Medicine at the University of Southern California School of Medicine. From 1963 to 1974, he was medical director of the Division of Adolescent Medicine at Children's Hospital in Los Angeles. Dr. Garell has served as president of the Society for Adolescent Medicine, chairman of the youth committee of the American Academy of Pediatrics, and as a forum member of the White House Conference on Children (1970) and White House Conference on Youth (1971). He has also been a member of the editorial board of the *American Journal of Diseases of Children.*

C. Everett Koop, M.D., Sc.D., is former Surgeon General, deputy assistant secretary for health, and director of the Office of International Health of the U.S. Public Health Service. A pediatric surgeon with an international reputation, he was previously surgeon-in-chief of Children's Hospital of Philadelphia and professor of pediatric surgery and pediatrics at the University of Pennsylvania. Dr. Koop is the author of more than 175 articles and books on the practice of medicine. He has served as surgery editor of the *Journal of Clinical Pediatrics* and editor-in-chief of the *Journal of Pediatric Surgery*. Dr. Koop has received nine honorary degrees and numerous other awards, including the Denis Brown Gold Medal of the British Association of Paediatric Surgeons, the William E. Ladd Gold Medal of the American Academy of Pediatrics, and the Copernicus Medal of the Surgical Society of Poland. He is a chevalier of the French Legion of Honor and a member of the Royal College of Surgeons, London.